INTRODUCTION TO CINE

Introduction to
CINE

SECOND EDITION

by

H. A. POSTLETHWAITE

FOUNTAIN PRESS - LONDON

First published 1958

Reprinted 1960

© 1958

FOUNTAIN PRESS, 46–47 CHANCERY LANE, LONDON, W.C.2

Made and printed in Great Britain by
The Garden City Press Limited
Letchworth, Hertfordshire

CONTENTS

FOREWORD

THE AIM of this book is to tell anyone who has never used a cine camera the things he or she needs to know: how to handle a cine camera, how to look after it, how to get good results from the outset, and how to project them to best advantage. It also explains in simple language how the camera and projector work, so even if you have already started with cine, you will find here advice to help to better results.

A lot has been happening to amateur filming: the cine camera has become more popular than ever; most people now choose 8 mm. in preference to 16 mm. or 9·5 mm.; colour has almost ousted black-and-white for outdoor filming; electric-eye cameras make filming almost automatic; and many people find further enjoyment by adding sound to their pictures. This second edition has been completely revised to take account of these things.

It isn't a textbook or treatise on film making. It is a practical, easy-to-read introduction to a fascinating hobby, designed to answer the whys and hows of the beginner, whether he wants to film everyday happenings with the least possible trouble, or aims at more 'serious' filming with the least possible expense. For filming can be as easy as taking snapshots with a still camera, and it need be no more expensive.

Chapter 1

FILMING IS FUN

THE DIFFERENCE between an ordinary snapshot and a cine picture is that whereas the 'still' camera shows what a thing or a person or a group of people looked like at a given instant, the cine film can show why, and how, and when, and where, as well as what. It can show cause as well as effect, and consequence too. Instead of a frozen smile, it gives us a burst of merriment – beginning, middle and end.

So many snapshots have to be explained before their significance can be appreciated. Look at the 'still' of children playing in the street (page 10). Without some explanation it is incomplete, but in fifteen seconds of screen time the cine camera could tell not only what the boy was doing, but how he came to be doing it, and why and when and how the little girls reacted. And the picture of the terrier and lawn-mower (page 11) does no more than hint at his amusing performance, whereas a few seconds of action would show it.

To take another example, let us suppose you have a picture of the family, rather exhausted, struggling up a steep and rocky path, little sister being helped forward by bigger sister, mother dragging behind a bit. You yourself are not in the picture because you were pressing the button. 'That's how we looked just before we got to the top', you explain.

A cine camera would bring the scene to life and explain it much more vividly without any words at all. It would show the progress of the climb, one or two amusing mishaps, the expressions on the faces of members of the party, in close-up, and ultimate success. The film would include you, too, for the cine camera has a shutter which permits the operator to walk into the picture. Even without this it would be easy

Fig. 1. This snapshot is rather meaningless without explanation. It needs a short cine sequence for the audience to grasp what it is all about.

to convey the impression that you were with the others by the simplest of cine devices, thus: the camera would portray the family panting up the steep path, pausing, then looking back and laughing.

At this point another shot would be cut in (the camera being held for this by, say, your wife) showing you making very hard going of the ascent. This shot (or 'scene') would be quite short, lasting only three or four seconds, but it would bring you in. Then would follow a continuation of the earlier scene, one of the party taking a couple of paces back and holding out a helping hand. This would be taken by you at the same time as the first shot. Finally we would see the helping hand actually pulling you up a bit of the path, Mother again pressing the button. All members of the party would thus be shown, apparently together, and the photographer ('cameraman')

Fig. 2. In this snapshot, too, 'frozen' action tells only part of the story. Film would bring the incident to life.

would remain anonymous, which of course he should be.

The slogan for cine is, '*Somebody doing something*'. Not 'Somebody going to do something', or 'Somebody having done something'. 'Action' is the word the director uses on the film set, and action is what makes cine interesting. Action, not just movement, for movement without action can appear purposeless and become rather boring. Movement always attracts the eye, but it will hold the attention only if it has significance – if it tells us something.

Nowhere is it more true than in cine that actions speak louder than words. If you recall the old silent pictures you will remember that when they included captions to explain the course of the story the captions were sometimes unnecessary and often irritating. It is not difficult to make a silent film that will explain itself completely without any words at all; even the name of the place where it was taken and the date may be conveyed by introducing something which indicates these things. And the trifling ingenuity needed to work in facts of this sort, as though by accident, adds to the fun.

Yes, it can be great fun making even a very simple picture of family life, or of a holiday, or of any interesting incident such as a wedding or a gala or fête. It may be a straightforward chronological record, projected just as it comes back from the processing station, or almost so. Or it may be trimmed and edited to give emphasis to the high spots and make the story flow more smoothly. It may even be a 'scripted' film, each sequence thought out in advance and the individual scenes planned so that the film progresses from a simple beginning to a definite conclusion that endows the whole with the quality of unity.

The actual handling of a cine camera need trouble no one; a cine camera is just as easy to use as a still camera. There is only one shutter speed for normal work; the correct exposure (i.e. lens aperture) can be found easily by means of a calculator or meter; many models have fixed-focus lenses, and with the others there is much greater latitude in focusing than with a still camera. In fact with some models there is nothing to do except point the camera at the subject and press the button. An 'electric eye' in the camera measures the light and automatically sets the lens for the correct exposure, and a small battery in the camera provides the motive power for the shutter and film transport.

Film is processed by the manufacturer, the cost as a rule being included in the price of the film, so the old-time Kodak slogan – 'You press the button, we do the rest' – really does apply. Cine is in fact the ideal form of photography for the busy man or woman who does not want to be bothered with anything more than that, but does want effective pictures. At the same time it can become an absorbing hobby, with immense opportunities for self-expression, interesting occupation for as much time as you care to devote to it, and a useful means of making new contacts and friendships.

Chapter 2

WHICH GAUGE?

THERE are three gauges of sub-standard film, 16 mm., 9·5 mm. and 8 mm. These measurements are of the overall width of the film; actual picture sizes are shown on page 14. The picture space of 16 mm. film is about one-tenth the size of a 35 mm. negative produced by a camera of the Leica type. The 9·5 mm. picture is a trifle smaller. The 8 mm. picture is a shade less than one-quarter the size of the 16 mm. picture; it measures one-fifth of an inch by one-seventh, and it is a thing to marvel at that so minute a transparency can be enlarged on the screen to a width of three or four feet and still be good to look at. A picture 3 ft. wide covers an area 36,000 times the area of the frame projected.

The camera is usually run by clockwork, and the film is ordinarily exposed (for silent pictures) at the rate of sixteen frames – i.e. separate pictures – per second. In between exposures the shutter cuts off the light coming through the lens while the exposed frame of the film is moved on and the next frame brought into position. The duration of this blackout is normally 1/32 sec., and the duration of each exposure 1/32 sec.

The amount of light reaching the film during the exposure is controlled by the size of the lens aperture, i.e. the size of the hole through which the light passes on its way to the film. On bright days the lens aperture is stopped down, i.e. made smaller, and in poor light it is opened up. With most cameras this is the only means of regulating the effective exposure given to the film, apart from the use of filters; but some films are fast, for use in poor light, and others slower for normal use.

And let me mention now, though I shall refer to it again later, that the 'f' number denoting the size of the lens aperture is

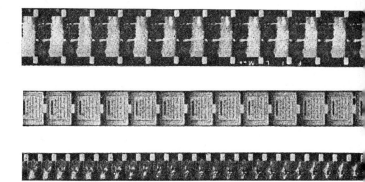

Fig. 3. 16 mm., 9·5 mm. and 8 mm. film.

higher when the aperture is small than when the aperture is big. F/16 is a *small* aperture for use in bright light; f/4·5 is a *big* aperture for relatively poor light.

With 16 mm. and 9·5 mm. film, the sixteen frames that are exposed in one second measure roughly 5 in.; more accurately, forty frames measure 1 ft. So 50 ft. of film will run, in the camera and in the projector, for just over two minutes. Two minutes isn't very long, but as the average duration of a 'shot' is only six seconds, a 50 ft. spool will be sufficient for twenty separate scenes.

You can of course get more scenes on a spool by limiting shots to four seconds each, and most of us tend to do this at first if we are acutely conscious of the cost of film stock. But the result will be jerky and irritating when projected. Conversely, if cost doesn't matter, we may tend to continue each scene longer than is necessary. That will certainly induce yawns unless there is drastic trimming, with consequent waste of material. On the whole it is best to stick to an *average* of six seconds per shot to begin with – and to learn to count six seconds fairly accurately, drawling silently to oneself as the motor runs: 'One and two and three and . . .'

Fifty feet of 8 mm. 'double-run' film lasts four times as long as 50 ft. of 16 mm. or 9·5 mm. film; but more about that later.

Fig. 4. 8 mm. double-run film.

The idea of six seconds for an average scene may cause you to lift your eyebrows if you have never thought about it before; but next time you are at the cinema count the number of seconds each scene lasts in a newsreel. You will be surprised.

A few more facts in brief: All cine cameras are daylight loading. If the film is bought on a spool, the metal sides of the spool protect the edges of the film from light; and the first (and last) few feet of film, which are not used for picture making, protect the usable film in between. This is because the film has an opaque backing, which also serves to prevent halation in the picture if bright objects are included.

As the film is exposed in the camera, it is wound off the spool on which it was supplied and on to a similar spool in the camera. The spool of the first film exposed then becomes the take-up spool for the next film. But as explained on page 24 8 mm. double-run film goes through the camera twice and finishes up on the spool on which it was to begin with.

If the film is bought in a magazine, for use in a camera designed for magazine loading, the film is completely protected by the casing of the magazine.

There is no need for a darkroom for cine work, unless you should become a cine addict and decide to process your films yourself. This is not difficult, but just a bit tedious.

All amateur film is non-inflammable.

The most popular films are 'reversal'; that is, the film taken from the camera is processed as a positive, ready to be projected. There are negative films, which are processed just as still camera films are, prints being made for projection on positive stock. But the 'neg-pos' process is not ordinarily used unless several copies of the film will be wanted.

15

Fig. 5. A snapshot taken with the normal lens of a still camera.
Compare this with the picture opposite.

Colour film is used in precisely the same way as black-and-white, without any modification of the camera and, apart from exceptional circumstances, without the addition of a filter.

Cine lenses are of relatively longer focal length than normal still camera lenses. This means that the distance from lens to film is greater *in relation to the size of the film* than in a still camera, with the consequence that the image falling on the film is bigger than it would otherwise be. So if you wanted to take, say, a head and shoulders close-up, and would have to stand with a still camera $3\frac{1}{2}$ ft. from the subject in order to fill the frame, you would get the same result with a cine camera at about 6 ft., and the 'drawing' would be better.

This is quite an advantage because both you and the subject will feel happier if you are separated by 6 ft. than if you are only $3\frac{1}{2}$ ft. apart; and in scenes which include several people,

Fig. 6. A cine camera with a normal lens, filming from the same viewpoint as the still camera that took the picture would show only this part of the scene, and thus bring the figures nearer.

such as a street incident, you will be less self-conscious if you can stand well back, in a doorway perhaps. Figs. 5 and 6 show the angle of view taken in by the normal lens of a still camera and by a cine camera.

Now to consider the relative merits of the three film sizes.

16 mm.

16 mm. gives the best quality, and if there is any possibility that you may some day want to take cine seriously, I advise that gauge from the outset. 'Seriously' means making pictures for educational or trade purposes, or perhaps for competition, or indeed for any purpose which might cause you to wish to project them to an audience outside the circle of family and friends.

Fig. 7. The Bell & Howell Autoload 16 mm. camera uses magazines which can be loaded into the camera in a second, even in sunlight. (See also fig. 29.)

If you think you might wish at some time in the future to make films to be shown on television, 16 mm. is certainly the gauge to choose. But 16 mm. apparatus and materials are more expensive than for the other gauges, and this has doubtless been the chief reason for the swing in favour of 8 mm. in recent years. However, you should certainly start with the size you intend to go on with.

16 mm. cameras are necessarily larger, and usually heavier, than those for 9·5 mm. or 8 mm. Some take 100 ft. spools (and film is cheaper in 100 ft. lengths); some others take 50 ft. magazines which are bought ready charged and sent off for processing as they are taken from the camera. Film in magazines costs more than on spools, but cameras taking magazines are compact and light and a partly used magazine can be removed (e.g. to change from colour to black and white) and reinserted without the loss of a single frame.

But although new 16 mm. cameras are expensive, it is possible to use that gauge economically if one is determined to have top quality with a minimum outlay. In fact there are amateurs who say they use 16 mm. because they can't afford 8 mm.! Partly because of the trend towards the smaller size, second-hand 16 mm. cameras can sometimes be picked up quite cheaply, even for as little as £10, and though such a camera may be twenty or thirty years old, if it was sturdily built it will still give many years of good service.

Similarly second-hand silent projectors can often be obtained for a few pounds. Their performance will not match up with that of modern instruments, but they will give good pictures on a moderately-sized screen. There is little demand for apparatus of this kind, and bargains can be found from time to time in the small advertisements in *Amateur Cine World*.

The enthusiast resolved to use 16 mm. cheaply buys ex-forces' 'disposal' film which can be got for a few shillings per hundred feet. He processes it himself, or sends it to a firm that specialises in the job. This makes 16 mm. filming in black and white very cheap indeed; and home processing is not difficult, though without enthusiasm it is likely to become tedious. Film bought in this way is usually time-expired, but when experience has been gained and some allowance made in exposure and processing, results can be substantially as good as those obtained on fresh film costing ten times as much. There is no

Fig. 8. Bell & Howell Model 627, twin-turret 16 mm. camera taking 100 ft. spools. The film is self-threading and the motor runs for 80 seconds without rewinding.

'disposal' colour film, and home processing of colour would be too much of a problem for most amateurs.

Disposal film is not available in 8 mm. or 9·5 mm., so this kind of economy is not possible with the smaller gauges. In any case with 8 mm. the slitting of the film with precision would be an almost insurmountable difficulty.

Thus the 16 mm. gauge may be the choice of the beginner with not much money but lots of enthusiasm, content with black-and-white filming, determined to get top quality in his work from the outset and hoping to progress to better apparatus later. Or it may suit the more casual film maker who wants the clearest possible picture with the least possible trouble.

The 16 mm. gauge would certainly be chosen by the worker who must have professional quality, regardless of expense or trouble, and who wishes to add sound on the film. His camera with accessories might cost several hundred pounds, and his projector about the same. But he will possibly not be working on his own just for the fun of the thing; more probably his filming will be sponsored by an institution or commercial undertaking.

9·5 mm.

This is an older gauge than 8 mm. It was very popular before the war when, by processing one's own film, cine could be very cheap indeed. Second-hand cameras and projectors are still obtainable at low prices, and new apparatus is also quite reasonably priced. With the Prince camera (fig. 9) and Princess projector (fig. 76) Pathescope have made provision for taking and projecting stills as well as cine. 'Colour transparencies at $\frac{3}{4}$d. each,' is their slogan.

At its best the projected picture with 9·5 mm. is almost as good as 16 mm., and the bigger frame as compared with 8 mm. does of course make for a clearer image. When it is not at its best there is a certain unsteadiness due perhaps to the arrangement of the sprocket holes down the centre of the film. But 9·5 mm. users are enthusiastic in defence of their chosen gauge.

One advantage of 9·5 mm. is that there are plenty of library

Fig. 9. The Pathescope Prince 9·5 mm. camera, designed for 'still' pictures (at a cost of ¾d. each) as well as cine.

films available, sound and silent, and hire charges are relatively cheap. The gauge would doubtless be more popular if colour film were as cheap as it is for 8 mm. Unfortunately it costs almost as much as 16 mm. film. Black-and-white film is cheaper, but not as cheap as 8 mm.

Many 9·5 mm. cameras take chargers which are slipped into the camera in the same way as 16 mm. magazines. Chargers may be sent away for processing, or they may be reloaded at home (in the dark) with a small saving of cost. Other 9·5 mm. cameras take spools or special magazines.

8 mm.

This gauge has become the choice of most amateurs. It has long held the field in America, and is firmly established in Australia, New Zealand and Africa; in Britain its popularity has increased greatly in recent years. The vast majority of new cine cameras sold are 8 mm.

The chief reason for this is its relative cheapness. 8 mm. film is less than one-third the price of 16 mm. for the same screen time; the cost per shot with an 8 mm. camera is in fact less than the cost of a snapshot or colour slide made with a still camera. 8 mm. cameras and projectors are also a great deal cheaper than those for 16 mm. The cameras are smaller, lighter

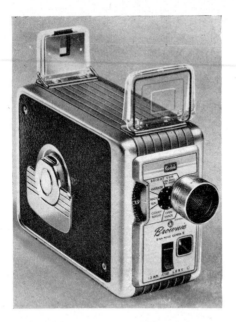

Fig. 10. Kodak Brownie model II 8 mm. camera with f/1·9 fixed-focus lens, easy to handle, inexpensive, but productive of excellent results.

and less noticeable; projectors are easier to transport and quieter; the Brownie projector (fig. 75) weighs only 9 lbs. all in. This may be quite an important consideration if you are likely to want to show films at the homes of friends.

Many 8 mm. cameras are so compact that they can be operated in one hand, though generally it is better to use both hands and best of all a tripod or other firm support. Nevertheless some of them include refinements which were formerly only to be found in the more expensive 16 mm. cameras.

The focal length of the normal lens in an 8 mm. camera is very short ($\frac{1}{2}$ in. or less) and consequently there is great depth of field (see p. 66); that means that even with a big aperture it is easy to get sharp focus on objects both near at hand and farther away without adjustment. The lens is often of fixed focus and so designed that everything is sharp from about 6 ft. onwards.

Projection reels for 8 mm. film are smaller, lighter, and more convenient to store than the other sizes; and storage of a number of the larger 16 mm. reels can become a problem. Home-made films of your family and of the town where you live are ideal for circulating to friends, particularly those overseas; they can say so much more than a letter or a snapshot. 8 mm. film can be bought in places where the other gauges would be unobtainable; and Kodachrome colour film is as cheap as Kodak black-and-white film.

One other point: several 8 mm. projectors make provision for linking a tape recorder in synchronism, either directly or by means of a linking unit. There is at least one 8 mm. projector which permits sound to be recorded magnetically on the film itself and reproduced in perfect synchronisation as the film is shown.

Those are the advantages of the smallest gauge, which 16

Fig. 11. Bell & Howell 8 mm. Autoset. An 'electric eye' automatically sets the lens to the correct aperture, and the large viewfinder gives a life-size image of the picture.

mm. users derisively term 'bootlace'. Now for the disadvantages: Although cameras and projectors are so much smaller and lighter, the film itself is somewhat less convenient to handle because the frames cannot well be examined without a magnifying glass. When the film is projected the degree of magnification is so great that any defects, such as specks of dust or scratches, show up badly. For the same reason it is best to restrict the width of the screen to about 3 ft. in the home; in a small hall, where the audience will be farther away from the screen, a picture 6 ft. wide will be satisfactory, provided the projector is powerful enough.

The big degree of magnification also rules out very fast black-and-white film, such as Kodak Tri-X, because the grain of the film would show up badly; but slow or medium speed film is fast enough for all normal occasions. You cannot hire talking films on 8 mm., as you can with the other gauges, but there are plenty of silent films to be obtained from the film libraries. Hiring charges are lower than for 16 mm., and printed films, such as those of Mickey Mouse, are relatively cheap to purchase.

Summing up, 8 mm. is ideal for family and holiday filming; it can be used with care for more serious work, but for commercial or educational purposes, and at other times when quality is all-important, 16 mm. is better. 8 mm. is not normally used for television, though it has been used when the only record of some important happening has been made by an amateur on 8 mm.

Most 8 mm. cameras take double-run spools of 25 ft. The film is similar to that used in 16 mm. cameras except that it has twice the number of perforations. It is exposed in the camera so that half the width is used at a time; when the first half has been exposed, the film is turned round and exposures made on the second half. After processing the film is slit down the middle by the processing station and the two parts joined together. This gives one length of 50 ft., and as each frame is only half the height of a 16 mm. frame, that length will run in the projector for twice as long as 50 ft. of 16 mm. film. Thus

25 ft. of double-run film gives the same screen time as 100 ft. of 16 mm. or 9·5 mm. film – just over four minutes.

A few cameras take single-run film or magazines, but whereas double-run spools can be bought almost anywhere, the other types are not so generally stocked by dealers and chemists.

8 mm. is at its best when filming subjects fairly close to the camera; in distant scenes detail is sometimes lacking; but if this induces the beginner to concentrate on close-ups and medium shots, so much the better. These are always more interesting and effective than views of the distant scene.

Chapter 3

HOW THE CAMERA WORKS

THE ESSENTIAL parts of a cine camera are: the lens, with its aperture and (optional) focusing controls; the mechanism for moving the film forward at 16 frames per second (and perhaps other speeds) and exposing the film to the light coming through the lens; the spools, magazine, or charger for holding the film before and after exposure; the viewfinder; and the footage counter, showing how much of a length of film has been used. There may be refinements, and these will be indicated in the next chapter, but the easiest way to explain how the camera works is to examine a simple model in detail.

Figs. 12 and 13 show the Kodak BB Junior, a spool-loading 16 mm. camera which has few frills and displays the essentials clearly. 8 mm. and 9·5 mm. cameras are basically similar, so if you follow the working of this simple 16 mm. camera, you will understand how any cine camera works. You may not be able to buy a BB Junior new, but there are plenty of second-hand models to be had in good condition, and a camera of this type can sometimes be picked up for as little as ten or fifteen pounds.

The camera takes 50 ft. spools. This size of 16 mm. spool has much to commend it for occasional filming. Film is relatively cheaper on 100 ft. spools, but 100 ft. cameras are necessarily bigger and heavier, and it is often inconvenient to wait until the 100 ft. length has been used up before seeing the pictures taken at the beginning of the length. The Kodak model K and the earlier model B are 100 ft. spool-loading cameras of similar design to the BB Junior.

Fig 12 shows all the external controls. The lens A has a built-in lenshood, which is a good feature. Focusing is done

26

Fig. 12. The Kodak BB junior, a 16 mm. spool-loading camera.
A—Lens with built-in lenshood.   D—Exposure button.
B—Lens mount.   E—Winding Key.
C—Lens aperture indicator.   F—Viewfinder.

by rotating the lens mount B; the figure for 25 ft. is engraved in red to indicate that when the camera is set for this distance everything will normally be sharp from 8 ft. onwards.

Many cameras, including some models of the BB Junior, have a fixed-focus lens. Most 8 mm. cameras are of fixed focus. This means that the lens has been permanently set at a focus which makes everything sharp from about 6 ft. on. It cuts out the trouble of focusing, but such lenses are not quite as fast as focusing lenses; that is to say, they do not open up to quite so large an aperture. For subjects nearer than 6 ft. a portrait attachment is slipped in front of the lens, or it may be built into the camera so that it is brought into action by moving a lever.

C in fig. 12 is the pointer which indicates the lens aperture, or 'stop', and here it may be useful to explain what a stop is, and the meaning of the symbol 'f'.

The amount of light passing through the lens is usually regulated by an affair of thin metal leaves between the front and rear glasses of the lens. This is called an iris diaphragm, because it works something like the iris of an eye. As the pointer C is moved, the aperture in the diaphragm is made larger or smaller; the bigger the aperture, the more light reaches the film, and the brighter the picture. But too much light will give a faint, washy picture.

The size of the opening, or stop, is distinguished by an 'f' number, and the 'f' value is obtained by dividing the diameter of the aperture into the focal length of the lens, which is the distance between the lens and the film. If the diameter of the lens opening is 1 in., and the focal length of the lens 4 in. (as in some still cameras) the aperture is f/4; similarly when the focal length of the lens is 1 in. (as in the BB camera) an aperture of $\frac{1}{4}$ in. diameter is still f/4. In both cases the value of the light reaching the film will be the same.

When the 'f' number is low (e.g. f/2·8) the aperture is fairly well open; so f/2·8 is termed a big stop, and conversely f/16 is a small stop. We 'stop down' to f/16 if the day is so bright that we have to restrict the amount of light reaching the film. We 'open up' to f/2·8, or some other big aperture, when the light is poor.

'F' numbers run in series, such as:

f/2, f/2·8, f/4, f/5·6, f/8, f/11, etc.,

or:

f/2·5, f/3·5, f/5, f/7, f/10, etc.,

or:

f/2·2, f/3·2, f/4·5, f/6·3, f/9, f/12·5, etc.

Each stop passes half the light passed by the preceding stop

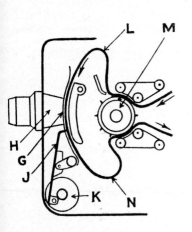

Figs. 13 and 14. Inside the
Kodak BB Junior: G—Gate;
H—Shutter position; J– Claw;
K—Rotating disc governing
the claw movement; L—Up-
per loop; M—Sprocket wheel;
N—Lower loop.

in the same series. So f/8 passes half the light of f/5·6, and one-quarter the light of f/4. In common parlance f/8 is one stop slower than f/5·6, and two stops slower than f/4 (see page 140).

To put it another way, the amount of light passing through the lens varies inversely as the square of the 'f' number.

D in fig. 12 is the exposure button. This is held down while pictures are being taken. If it is pressed hard down, it will stay

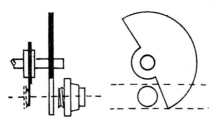

Fig. 15. The shutter, which rotates between the lens and the gate.

down until it is pushed up again. This permits the cameraman to walk into the picture if he wants to, but of course the camera must be on a really firm support when it is left to work unattended.

E is the key for winding up the motor; when the spring is fully wound the camera will run for about thirty seconds before it needs rewinding. But it is a good plan to rewind after each shot. This keeps the camera always at the ready and avoids the risk of the motor running down in the middle of a lengthy shot taken on the spur of the moment. It is better, however, not to leave the spring fully wound if the camera is to be put away without use for any length of time.

F is the viewfinder. On the front lens of the viewfinder two lines are engraved marked '6 ft.' and '2 ft.' When pictures are being taken nearer than 6 ft., the top of the subject must be kept below the appropriate line, because the camera lens is a couple of inches lower than the viewfinder and 'sees' a lower image. This is termed correction for parallax. The way in which correction is made differs in other cameras; if for example the viewfinder were at the side of the camera instead of on top, correction would be made horizontally, not vertically.

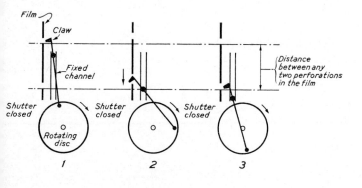

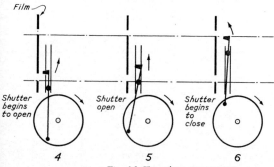

Fig. 16. The claw movement.
1 and 2—the claw pulls down the film; 3—the claw is withdrawn;
4 and 5—it is pulled upwards ready for its next grab; 6—it is pushed
forward into the next pair of sprocket holes on the film.

On the top of the camera there is a footage scale. This shows
how much of the 50 ft. spool of film remains unexposed. It
is actuated by a feeler which responds to the varying thickness
of the spool of film in the camera, and it is usually not very
precise. This does not matter once you get to know your
camera and remember that when the indicator says, for
example, that there are 5 ft. left, there are really 10 ft. On some
cameras the film counter is geared to the mechanism and
records the footage that has been exposed, or even the number

31

of frames. This can be very useful for expert work, but the BB type of footage scale is good enough for most purposes.

Now to look inside the camera (figs. 13 and 14).

As already said, each frame of the film is exposed for 1/32 sec. and then the light coming through the lens is cut off by the

Fig. 17. A 16 mm. daylight loading spool.

shutter for 1/32 sec. while that frame is replaced in the 'gate' G of the camera by the next frame. The shutter, which is hidden away in the place marked H in fig. 14, is a rotating disc of which half has been cut away (fig. 15).

The film is moved on by a claw, J, which is actuated by the rotating disc, K, in such a way that the claw pulls down the film (1 and 2) and is withdrawn (3), is pushed upwards ready for its next grab (4 and 5), and is pushed forward into the next pair of sprocket holes on the film (6) (fig. 16).

To protect the film from damage by this snatching and grabbing, it is formed into a loop, L, before it comes to the gate. A sprocket wheel, M, passes the film forward from the supply spool at precisely the speed at which it will go through the gate, and the same sprocket wheel takes up the film after exposure, via another loop, N, and passes it on to the take-up spool.

To load the camera, the film from the supply spool is threaded so that it follows the course ready drawn in the camera (see fig. 13) – the emulsion side (white) being of course nearest to the lens – and is attached to the take-up spool. In some spools the centre hole is square on one side (as in fig. 17) and round on the other, so that it is impossible to put it in the camera the wrong way round.

Fig. 18. The claw mechanism. The claw is at the end of its downward pull—position 2 in fig. 16. The spring near the claw is to hold it back while the film is being loaded into the camera.

With the film threaded the mechanism is run for a second or two with the camera open, to see that the loops are correctly maintained; then the lid is put on the camera, and it is run again for eight seconds to use up the 'leader'.

Each 50 ft. spool of film actually contains 58 (or more) ft. The first 5 ft. and the last 3 ft., termed 'leader' and 'trailer', are provided to protect the rest during daylight loading and unloading. They are cut off by the processing station, so any exposures that might be made on them would be lost. But as the leader and trailer can only give limited protection, the camera must always be loaded and unloaded with care, in subdued light, preferably indoors.

That explains the mechanism of this 16 mm. camera, and though other models vary in detail the general principle is the same. In an 8 mm. or 9·5 mm. camera there may not be a sprocket wheel, loops being provided by some other device; or there may not even be any loops with the narrower and shorter 8 mm. film. In magazine cameras the mechanism of film transport is largely or wholly incorporated in the magazine.

The clockwork machinery of the camera is sealed by the makers and should not be meddled with. The gate can be taken apart, or opened, for cleaning, but there is little else to be done by way of maintenance, except to keep the camera absolutely free from dust and damp.

Chapter 4

CHOOSING A CAMERA

THE DESCRIPTION in chapter 3 of a simple 16 mm. camera has indicated the essential features of any cine camera and explained how it functions. But many modern cameras have modifications which make the camera easier to use or extend its scope. Of course the more numerous the special features, the higher the cost, and if the camera is to be used only for family and holiday filming, a simple and moderately-priced camera will do all you are likely to require. You can always trade in the simple camera in part-exchange for a more advanced model as you progress. But it is useful to know what refinements are available.

The Lens: While a fixed-focus lens can be perfectly satisfactory for family filming, a lens which can be focused will give sharper results in poor light and at close quarters. The bigger the aperture to which a lens can be opened, the higher the cost; a lens of f/1·4 will cost quite a lot more than one of f/2·8; it passes four times as much light, but there is no sense in paying for this facility unless you are likely to need it.

The aperture in most cameras is regulated by an iris diaphragm (see page 28), but in some cameras there may be, instead of the iris diaphragm, a metal disc with holes of various sizes which control the amount of light reaching the films. Perfectly satisfactory, but you may only be able to work at the marked apertures; if these are f/2·8, f/4, f/5·6 and so on, you can't get in between for f/3·5. But the nearest marked number (f/4 in this case) will be quite suitable.

In many cameras lenses are interchangeable, which can be an advantage; in others there is a turret holding two or three lenses so that you can change instantly from a normal lens to

Fig. 19. Paillard Bolex H16M is one of the most popular 16 mm. cameras. It incorporates full parallax compensation down to 1½ ft., has a zoom-type viewfinder and provision for electric motor drive.

a wide-angle or long-focus lens; this is very convenient, but such cameras are less compact than those with single lenses and, of course, cost more.

A point to be noted is that when you change from the normal lens to one of the others, you do not change the perspective of the picture unless you change your standpoint. With the camera in the same position the perspective is the same whatever lens you use. The wide-angle lens takes in more of the scene, and the long focus (or telephoto) lens less, thus giving a smaller or larger image of the central part. (See figs. 21–23.)

The modern tendency in single-lens cameras is to use a wider angle than formerly; the 16 mm. camera often has a lens of 20 mm. focal length instead of 25 mm. (1 in.), and the 8 mm. camera a lens of 10 mm. instead of 12 or 13 mm. These wider angle lenses would take in an area rather greater than that

Fig. 20. The Eumig Servomatic 8 mm. camera has fully-automatic exposure control, electric drive and remote control release; a photoelectric unit sets the aperture and a small flash-lamp battery supplies power for film transport.

shown in fig. 22, but less than the fig. 21 scene. They have somewhat greater depth of field so that it is easier to get sharp definition over all; on the other hand, if you want a good close-up, you must take the camera nearer to the subject.

For a few cameras Zoom lenses are available as an extra – that is lenses with variable focal length; they are expensive.

Electric-eye Cameras: An increasing number of cameras incorporate a photo-electric meter which measures the light and adjusts the lens aperture automatically or semi-automatically for correct exposure. In the automatic camera, having set an indicator to the correct film speed (see page 49) you merely point the camera at the subject and press the button. Other cameras incorporate exposure calculators (see fig. 29). One or two cameras include electric drive; a small flash-lamp battery works the motor and saves the trouble of winding up – and remembering to do so. It also permits continuous filming; whereas a clockwork motor will only run for, perhaps, 30 seconds on one winding, the electric motor will keep going as

Figs. 21, 22, 23. These pictures show the different aspects of the same scene filmed through the three lenses of turret cameras, such as those shown in figs. 24 and 25. The centre picture is what would be produced by the normal lens; the wide-angle lens would take in more, as in the top picture; and a long focus or telephoto lens would include only the portion shown in the bottom picture, the standpoint being the same in each case.

Fig. 24. The turret version of the Bell & Howell 8 mm. Autoset, a similar camera to that shown in fig. 11 but with three lenses of differing focal length.

long as you like. But some spring-driven motors have a device to indicate when the motor needs rewinding.

The Shutter: If a camera has one filming speed it will be 16 frames per second (or 18 f.p.s. in some newer cameras) but many cameras have variable filming speeds of 8, 12, 16, 24, 32 and 64 f.p.s., or some of these. When a fast filming speed is used, such as 64 f.p.s., the picture will appear in slow-motion when projected (because the 64 frames exposed in one second will occupy four seconds on the screen). Filming at 8 f.p.s. gives speeded-up motion, and can be amusing, but this speed is useful when the lighting is poor and the people being filmed can be persuaded to make all movements a bit more slowly than usual.

Variable *shutter* speeds are sometimes provided. This means that without changing the normal *filming* speed of 16 f.p.s., the shutter can be adjusted to reduce the amount of light it passes to the film. By this means sharper pictures can be obtained of fast-moving objects, without slow-motion, and scenes can be effectively faded-in and faded-out. Other shutter refinements are single-frame filming (useful for making an animated or cartoon film and for trick titles); time exposures with single-frame filming; provision for a cable release; provision for back-winding the film so that after a scene has been filmed the same length of film can be put through a second time in order to superimpose a title, or to superimpose a fade-in of a scene on top of the fade-out of the previous shot, thus creating a 'lap-dissolve'.

The Viewfinder: An accurate viewfinder is most important in order that you can see, while you are filming, precisely the area of the scene taken in by the camera lens. There should therefore be correction for parallax (see page 30); if there isn't, you will have to make mental allowance at short distances. If you wear spectacles it will be important that you can see a clear image through the finder; in some cases special eyepieces can be fitted to compensate for defective eyesight. A few cameras have provision for viewing the scene through the actual taking lens. If the camera has a turret head and more than one lens, either a separate finder should be fitted for each, or the finder should be adjustable. In a few cases a finder of the Zoom type may be fitted.

Footage Counter: The method used described on page 31 of measuring the amount of film used is not very accurate, and a geared counter is more commonly fitted. There may be in addition a frame counter, which shows the number of frames actually exposed; this is useful in conjunction with a rewind when superimposing one scene on another.

In the light of that list of special features (and you may feel that you need few of them to begin with) and having decided how much you want to spend, the next thing is to consider how to set about selecting a camera.

If a new camera is contemplated and if it is of well-known make, a lot can be taken for granted; if the model has been on sale in this country for two or three years and has earned a good reputation, that is certainly to its credit. There may be an element of chance in buying a foreign-made camera only recently put on the market unless it is backed by a world-famous name; and with all foreign-made cameras it is as well to make sure that there are satisfactory arrangements in this country for service if anything should go wrong.

The size and weight of the camera are rather obvious points to mention. It is all very well to hold an impressive-looking camera in the hand for a few minutes, slightly dazzled by its gleaming chromium plate and itching to try out this gadget and that, and say, 'Bit heavy, but I can manage it'. Its weight and bulk may not matter when you are actually using it; but they may become deciding factors when you hesitate between taking the camera on an excursion and leaving it at home.

It is better to start with a camera of modest size, with no

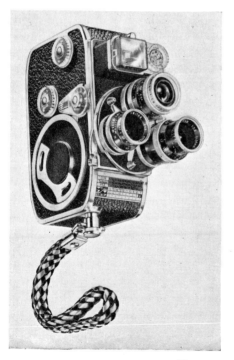

Fig. 25. Paillard Bolex D8L, an advanced 8 mm. camera with 3-lens turret, is unique in that a photo-electric cell is situated behind the taking lens and thus measures the light that will actually reach the film, whichever lens is used. Among other features are variable filming speeds, variable shutter, zoom-type viewfinder, automatic-geared footage counter, single frame exposures, provision for a cable release and a 7 ft. film run.

more refinements than you know you will need. For example, don't go in for a camera with a turret head and several lenses unless you are sure you can't get all you want with a single lens of normal focal length. Again, while it is pleasant to have a rangefinder which enables you to be certain the camera is focused with absolute accuracy on the principal object in view, this refinement is really useful only when using long-focus lenses.

If you look through the lists of winners in amateur cine competitions, such as the *Amateur Cine World* 'Ten Best' competition, you will find that simple cameras picked up second-hand at very low prices can produce work of the highest standard. In cine, even more than in still photography, the man behind the camera is more important than the camera itself.

If it is proposed to buy a second-hand camera, it is wise to arrange to have it on trial, or with a money-back guarantee, and if possible to consult someone who is familiar with cine cameras.

A careful examination should be made, inside and outside, for traces of rust and for any accumulation of dirt that might cause trouble. The catch on the door of the camera should be tested to make sure it fastens securely. If the camera is magazine loading, be sure it takes standard magazines, unless you are prepared to load the magazines yourself and can get a sufficient number for use. If the camera is foreign made and is being bought from a private owner, there should be some evidence that customs duty has been paid.

The camera should be wound fully, preferably with a length of waste film in it, to see that it runs sweetly, without bumps or judders, and without slowing down, for something like half a minute. The loops of film should be maintained – that is, neither loop should get bigger or smaller – and there should be no scratches on the film after it has been run through.

The lens should be removed from the camera if possible and examined to see that there are no serious scratches and not much dust between the components, and that there is no indication that cemented components are separating. Tiny bubbles in the glass are unimportant.

The next test should be to make a mark on a length of waste film threaded in the camera at the top of the upper loop, or just before it enters the gate; to run the camera for exactly ten seconds; and then to measure the film that has passed through the gate. It should be 4 ft. (2 ft. with 8 mm. film) if the camera is making sixteen exposures per second.

If the camera passes these tests, a full length of film should be exposed in a series of shots, using a really rigid tripod or other firm support for the camera. Some of the shots should be on fairly near subjects, some on subjects at about 12 ft., and others at greater distances. Some should be in poor light (e.g. in the shade) so that a big aperture is used; but care should be taken to expose freely all sides of the camera itself to sunshine, so that if there is a light leak the film will show fogging. A record should be made of the aperture and the measured distance to the subject for each shot.

When the film is returned from processing it should be projected to check that (1) all shots are in sharp focus; (2) all are steady, i.e. they do not float up and down or from side to side; (3) there is no fluctuation in the density of the picture within the same scene; and (4) there is no fogging. Fogging might show up on monochrome film as a white haze over a few frames, or as occasional flashes of white on the screen. With colour film fogging causes reddish patches.

If a friend has been enlisted to superintend these first shooting efforts, he should be asked to view the projected result. He may be able to see things that you would not regard as significant.

If the camera proves satisfactory, start using it right away. Practise with an empty camera, and then with film in it at varying distances and under varying conditions. Be critical of results, and listen attentively to the comments of friends and relatives. You are sure to make mistakes, and in the excitement of seeing your own work on the screen you may be disposed to be more generous in excusing them than you ought

42

to be. As each fault is brought home to you, practise still further to avoid it.

This doesn't mean that every shot that is less than perfect must be scrapped. Far from it. In all probability 90 per cent. of your filming will be good enough to preserve even at the outset. But there is a good deal to learn before every shot can be regarded as technically perfect.

One of the best ways to learn how to get the best out of the camera is to join the local cine society and take part in its activities. There are hundreds of cine societies throughout the country and in America and the Commonwealth. Some are for 8 mm. users only. At all of them visitors are welcome. You will be able to see the work of other amateurs and compare its quality with that of your own films, and you will find experienced members delighted to advise on any difficulties and problems you may have met.

Chapter 5

CARE OF THE CAMERA

THERE ARE TWO precautions every camera-user ought to take from the outset. First, the camera should have a case, and the camera should be kept in it except when actually in use. The case may hold the camera only, or it may have space for spare spools or magazines of film, exposure meter, filters and other gadgets. It should preferably be strong enough to protect the camera from accidental damage such as might be caused by a bump or a fall; but here you are up against the difficulty that a really sturdy case, particularly if it holds accessories as well as the camera, will add to the bulk and weight to be carried about.

If you haven't got a case and don't want to buy one, a strong dustproof cardboard box is a reasonable substitute.

The second precaution is to insure the camera. It costs very little to do so – about 15s. per £100 – and this will cover theft, loss and accidental damage. Accessories such as exposure meter, tripod and the projector may be included in the sum insured if desired. It is a comforting feeling to know that if someone catches his foot against the tripod and brings the camera crashing down, you won't have to stand the racket yourself, and your friend won't suffer the embarrassment of feeling he ought to pay.

Of course insurance will not cover wear and tear, or damage due to neglect. Dust is an insidious enemy. Every time the camera is loaded it should be examined and dusted. It is sometimes a mystery how the dust gets in, but a careful scrutiny will almost always reveal some particles that ought not to be there. A camel-hair brush can be used to get them out of corners, but after a time brushes tend to shed bits of hair which

44

Fig. 26. The interior of the Bell & Howell 16 mm. model 627 (fig. 8).

may be as troublesome as any other form of dirt. It is safer to use a little gadget made specially for the purpose which blows the dust out.

Sometimes scraps of fluff get caught in the gate, with the result that there seems to be a bunch of foliage waving about when the picture is projected, usually at the top of the picture. This means that there is dirt at the *bottom* of the camera gate (unless it is in the projector gate), for the camera, of course, takes all pictures upside down.

The lens should be examined from time to time, being removed from the camera if provision is made for removal, and held up against the light for examination. Any dust should be blown away with the blower, or removed by means of one of the little brushes sold specially for the purpose. If the lens is still dirty it may be wiped gently with lens-cleaning tissue – the kind sold for photographic lenses, not the kind sold for spectacles. It should not be wiped with a handkerchief, or with silk, which would electrify the surface and actually attract dust. Needless to say the lens must never be touched with the fingers.

45

Fig 27. A typical interior of an 8 mm. camera, the Bell & Howell Sportster. The gate springs open automatically when the camera is opened. It will be noted that there are no sprockets.

If the lens should become really dirty, or if there is any indication that the cemented components are separating, it should be sent for repair by an expert. It is most unwise for the amateur to attempt to take a cine lens apart.

If the camera is being put away empty and is not likely to be used for some time, the motor should be allowed to run down and then wound up for three or four turns of the winding handle. It should not be left fully wound.

It is unwise to attempt to oil the camera. An excess of oil may easily cause as much trouble as lack of oil. If the motor does not run sweetly, it is best to consult a dealer and if necessary to have the defect put right by the makers. No attempt should be made to explore the parts of the mechanism that have been sealed by the manufacturer.

The take-up spool in the camera – and spare spools if any – should be safeguarded from damage. If the spool became bent the film might fail to wind on smoothly.

It is as well every now and again to take a critical look at the tripod. If it is made of wood, see that all screws are tight. If there are wing nuts brazed on to screws, see that they are not working loose. A nut that refuses to be tightened or untightened may render the tripod useless, and things like that always seem to happen at the most inconvenient time.

Chapter 6

EXPOSURE

PEOPLE who have been using cine cameras for years are sometimes hazy about the difference between overexposure and underexposure. They are never quite sure which way the fault has been if a picture is too dark or too light on the screen.

When a picture on reversal film is too dark, it didn't get enough light in the camera; it was underexposed; the lens aperture used was too small (see fig. 28). And a picture that is too light was overexposed.

If a length of reversal film were processed without any exposure at all it would come out black; and if it were thoroughly fogged with a great deal too much light it would come out as clear film.

When a photograph is taken with a still camera the effect of wrong exposure *in the negative* is the opposite of this; underexposure gives a thin negative, without detail in the shadows, and overexposure a dense negative. An overexposed negative can usually be made to yield a satisfactory print, but nothing can be done with a badly underexposed negative. So the still photographer's rule is: 'Always avoid underexposure'.

In cine work with reversal film (including colour) the rule is different. The overexposed film is too bright and detail has gone, but the underexposed film, although too dark, will still show some detail and will often be usable. So the cine worker's maxim is: 'Always avoid overexposure'.

The reason for this is simple. When reversal film (including colour film) is processed, it is first developed up as a *negative*, just as is the film from a still camera. The parts of the emulsion that have been affected by the light coming through the lens thus become black; the parts not affected (e.g. the heavy

Fig. 28. An example of underexposure. The lens aperture
used was too small, i.e. f/16 instead of f/8.

shadow parts of the image) remain white. At a later stage in the
processing the black parts of the emulsion are bleached, and
the parts that had remained white are developed up, yielding
a positive image ready for projection.

If the film has been overexposed, the first development
yields a negative with lots of black, all of which will be
bleached out, and the more black there is in the negative, the
less white remains to be developed up for the positive image.
So the overexposed film is weak and thin, detail being barely
discernible on the screen in a haze of overall brilliance. Really
excessive overexposure would of course give practically clear
film, everything having been developed up at the negative
stage and subsequently bleached away.

With underexposure, very little black image results from
the first development, so there is not much to be bleached;

but lots of white remains in the emulsion and this will become a dense image after the second development.

Exposure, as we have seen, is controlled by the lens aperture, and three things have to be taken into account when deciding what aperture to use for any given shot. They are, first, the speed of the film that is being used; second, the brightness of the light which reaches the film; and, third, the idiosyncrasies (if any) of the particular camera in use.

First, film speed. This is usually indicated on the carton, or in the instructions accompanying the film. If it isn't, the dealer will tell you the speed of the film you are buying, and it is really important to know this. The fastest reversal films are about sixteen times as fast as the slowest – a difference between f/12·5 and f/3·5 in the same light.

Unfortunately there are several different ways of quoting film speeds. A table showing how they compare is given on page 140. If your exposure meter is scaled for the standard arithmetical rating (ASA) as is probable, it is best to take this as a basis. ASA stands for American Standard Arithmetical, and this rating is almost always quoted on film cartons or in the instructions enclosed with the film. In this system, when the speed number is doubled the speed of the film is doubled; thus a film of ASA 100 is twice as fast as one of ASA 50.

Fig. 29. The exposure guide on the side of the Autoload camera (fig. 7).

49

Sometimes the film speed is quoted as, e.g., 'BS log. 25', or simply 'BS 25'. BS stands for British Standard – though the British and American Standards are the same – and in this logarithmetic notation the speed number is increased by 3 when the speed of the film is doubled. Thus BS 28 is double BS 25.

If this seems a bit confusing, well, stick to the ASA notation.

Continental films commonly quote a DIN rating, though the ASA equivalent is usually given too. The DIN rating is equal to the BS log rating minus 10. Thus DIN 15 equals BS 25, and an increase of 3 in the DIN rating indicates a doubling of the film speed.

Until Weston brought out their Master III model the most commonly used rating was that for the Weston meter. But whereas that used to be one degree less than the ASA rating, the Weston rating with their Master III model is the same as ASA. To quote a speed as, e.g., Weston 50 is therefore ambiguous: with the Master III model, Weston 50 means ASA 50; with the Master II and earlier models, Weston 50 means ASA 64.

The second factor governing exposure is the brightness of the light that strikes the film; that is, the light *reflected* by the subject being filmed, via the lens, to the film. This will depend partly on the sort of subject, and partly on whether it is a bright day or a dull day. A white face, for instance, will reflect more light than a black dog, but both will send more reflected light to the lens on a sunny day than on a cloudy day.

The thought that a face, or a dog, or anything else that is not self-luminous, is made visible to the camera, and to the eye too, by means of the light it reflects may seem novel at first. But a moment's consideration will show that it must be so. And in photography it is the intensity, and perhaps the colour, of the reflected light that we are concerned with.

In artificial light all black-and-white films are a little slower than in daylight, because artificial light is yellowish in comparison with daylight. The light reflected by objects viewed by artificial light has therefore a yellow tinge, and black-and-white film is less sensitive to yellow light than it is to the bluish-white light of daylight.

Fig. 30. In a shot like this, taken against the light, the exposure meter would be held close to the child and pointing downwards to ensure that the sun did not give too high a reading or the dark background too low a reading.

It follows that to get correct exposure we have to estimate for each shot the value of the reflected light reaching the lens, and then use a big stop, such as f/3·5, if that value is low, or a small stop, such as f/16, if there is a lot of light. There are two ways of estimating the value of the light: with the help of an exposure table or calculator, or by means of an exposure meter.

An exposure table is often given with the film, and some of these are excellent; some people use the table enclosed with Kodachrome film in preference to an exposure meter; and used intelligently in reasonably good light it should give uniformly correct results. This is not to decry other tables and calculators, but the Kodachrome one is particularly easy to understand and quick in action.

An excellent calculator, suitable for use with all types of films is also published in *Amateur Cine World* from time to time.

And, by the way, when an exposure table says the aperture should be 'f/5·6 – f/8' it means that the lens should be set half way between those markings. This applies where the aperture is controlled by an iris diaphragm, whether the lens has 'click stops' or not, but there are a few cameras where only the marked apertures can be used. In these cases it will generally be desirable to use the smaller of the two apertures named – f/8 in preference to f/5·6.

For outdoor scenes in reasonably bright light, then, a table or calculator will usually prove satisfactory, but it will not be so good indoors or when the light is poor. Here an exposure meter with a photo-electric cell to measure the light is needed. There are two kinds of these. One measures the light actually reflected from the subject to be filmed; the other measures the light falling on the subject, and from this measurement derives the value of the reflected light.

In the first case the 'reflected light' meter is pointed at the subject and the brightness value shown by the meter is related to the film speed. If the meter is specially designed for cine, the appropriate aperture can be read off at once. If the meter is designed for still photography, the aperture (at 16 f.p.s.) will be that shown for a shutter speed of 1/30 sec. When the camera has an electric eye, the camera itself serves as a reflected light-exposure meter, and it should be used in the same way as any other meter of that kind.

This is simplicity itself if the subject is more or less equally bright all over, but if parts are very bright and other parts very dark, a reading obtained by pointing the meter straight forward from the camera position may not give a good result. In the case of the white face and the black dog, for instance, the meter would probably take limited account of either; it would be influenced mainly by the background, giving a low reading if the background was dark and a high reading if the background was bright. So in that case it would be necessary to take a reading of the light value of the face, another reading for the dog (yes! even a black dog reflects light), and, ignoring the background, split the difference. But if the face mattered more than the dog, it would be desirable to use a light value nearer that taken from the face than that taken from the dog.

In fact with colour film it would be best to disregard the dog altogether and work on the meter reading for the face only. Colour film has less latitude than black-and-white film, and the flesh tones would be unsatisfactory if the aperture were more than half a stop bigger than that appropriate to the face reading.

If you hesitate to get close up in order to take a reading from the face of a subject, a reading can be taken from something else of approximately equal light value, such as the palm of the hand, holding your hand so that the light falling on it is similar to that falling on the face and from the same direction. But it is important to hold the meter so that it takes in only what you want it to take in, and does not cast a shadow on the thing it is measuring (see fig. 30).

When measuring the light for a long shot which includes the sky, it is usually best to tilt the meter slightly downwards so that it is not too much influenced by the brightness of the sky. If, however, the sky is the important feature of the scene, as it would be, for example, when filming a sunset, the foreground should be ignored and the meter pointed at the sky. The landscape would then be very much underexposed and would appear in silhouette, but this is quite satisfactory both in monochrome and in colour if the horizon is kept low in the frame.

The other kind of photo-electric meter, known as an incident light meter, does not measure the light reflected from the subject but the light falling on it. The window of the photo-electric cell, which is covered with a diffusing screen, is pointed towards the light source, and the reading applied as before. This gives the aperture appropriate to a scene of average brightness, on the principle that an average scene reflects a uniform fraction of the light falling on it.

It is often maintained that the reading obtained by the incident light method should be used for all subjects, so that scenes darker than average will appear appropriately dark on the

Fig. 31. The Weston Master III Cine Exposure meter. One of the most popular meters in the world, it gives direct readings over a wide brightness range. Designed primarily for reflected light readings, it can be adapted for use by the incident light method by the addition of the Invercone attachment.

Fig. 32. Weston meter with Invercone attachment in position. The 'Multiplier' is inserted when the light is very bright.

screen, and light scenes will appear light. In extreme cases, however, discretion must be used.

Cine users are about equally divided in preferring reflected-light and incident light meters, and equally emphatic in support of their views. Either type will give accurate exposures provided you learn how to use it to best advantage, studying carefully the instructions issued with the meter and applying common sense.

It is possible to use a reflected-light meter for incident light readings, and sometimes convenient to do so. The highest possible reading is taken from a sheet of white paper or card, about a foot square, and the lens is then set three stops wider than the meter says; e.g. if the meter says f/11, the lens is set at f/4 for an average subject. For a subject of light tone it would be sufficient to open up two stops, e.g. from f/11 to f/5·6. This method of taking a reading can be useful when the light is very poor; the needle may make no response when the meter is pointed at the subject to be filmed, but may give a useful reading from the sheet of white paper.

There are numerous photo-electric meters available from four or five pounds upwards. The Weston costs £9 odd, and several others sell at about the same price; some of these are amazingly light, neat and compact. Broadly, the difference between a low-priced meter and one costing more is that the dearer meter will be more sensitive to weak light. It is sound economy to buy the best you can afford, because there are sure to be occasions when you will want to film in poor light; and it is not much good having a lens with a big aperture if your meter won't tell you when it is safe to work fully opened up.

A final word about photo-electric meters: it is not unusual for two meters, even of the same make, to give differing readings. Don't conclude that there is something wrong with yours because it doesn't agree exactly with Bill's or Joe's. If it responds nicely at both ends of the scale, and in the middle, it is all right. All you need do is, Get to Know Your Meter.

In between the exposure calculator or table and the photo-electric meter there is the extinction type of meter, by means of

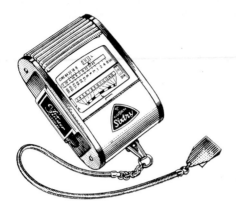

Fig. 33. The Sixtry is a moderately-priced exposure meter which gives direct readings for both cine and still photography by either the reflected light or incident light method.

which the light reflected from the scene is measured visually. In some models, which are quite cheap and extremely compact, a graduated screen is used to cut down the light until the eye can only just discern it; the appropriate aperture is then read off a calculator.

The drawback to this type of meter is that the eye is influenced to greater or less degree by external conditions so that it is liable to be less sensitive to the meter in bright light out of doors and more sensitive when used indoors or in poor light. Such meters when used with discretion can, however, be very useful.

The third factor which *may* govern exposure is the possibility that your camera may have some idiosyncrasy. Most probably it is quite normal, the shutter giving an exposure of 1/32 sec. at 16 f.p.s., and the lens apertures being marked accurately. But there is the chance that the shutter speed or the lens aperture markings may be a trifle out. The diameter of the lens opening at f/16, for example, with a 1 in. lens is only 1/16 in., and if instead of 1/16 in. the iris diaphragm closed down to 1/18 in., the lens would be about half a stop slow at that setting.

Whatever your camera, you must get to know it, and in the odd case allow for any peculiarity. It may be necessary to make allowances even with a quite expensive cine camera. With one such I found that when one of the three lenses on the turret was set at f/4·5, for example, the film was under-exposed in comparison with similar scenes filmed at the same aperture with the other lenses. It was therefore necessary to remember always to open up that lens by half a stop (e.g., to f/4) when the meter advised f/4·5.

A further incident may emphasise the point. A friend took a newly-acquired 8 mm. camera to Switzerland. The meter said that for a particular scene in the snow the correct aperture was f/22. The smallest marked aperture on the camera was f/16, but he found that by pushing the indicator a little further, he could get a smaller stop. He assumed this would be f/22 and exposed accordingly, but every shot was badly under-exposed. He had in fact closed down to something like f/45, and realised later that it was unsafe to make assumptions of that kind, or to try to use that camera at a smaller aperture than f/16 unless a neutral denisty, or other filter, were put on the lens (see page 71).

It is hardly necessary to say that if the camera has more than one filming speed, the duration of the shutter opening will vary with the number of frames exposed per second. At 8 f.p.s. (accelerated motion) the shutter will be open for 1/16 sec., so an aperture one stop smaller should be used (e.g. f/5·6 instead of f/4) than for 16 f.p.s. One consequence of this is that it is possible to film at 8 f.p.s. when the light is not good enough for 16 f.p.s.

At 24 f.p.s. the shutter is open for only 1/48 sec., requiring an aperture half a stop larger than for normal filming, and for 64 f.p.s. (slow motion filming) the lens must be opened up two stops more than would be used at 16 f.p.s.

Chapter 7

HOLDING THE CAMERA
STEADY

AS SOON as you begin to take a pride in the quality of your filming you will realize what a big difference there is between a picture that is rock steady and one that wavers. It is not the kind of thing the family is likely to comment on; they may notice that the steady picture is the better, but they probably won't know why, and they may be disposed to blame the camera or the projector when the fault is really yours.

I know the feeling that erecting a tripod, particularly with an 8 mm. camera, makes the business of filming seem too formal and may tend to spoil the spontaneous quality of the film. And nine out of ten users of 8 mm. cameras are content to hold the camera in the hand. But try the experiment of taking two shots of the same scene, one hand-held and the other with the camera supported absolutely firmly on a wall, or something equally unyielding, and look for the difference. Let the scene include the horizon, fairly high up in the picture space, or some other strong horizontal line not far from the top or bottom edge. Don't have much action in the scene, for interesting action rivets the attention and so tends to cover up faults.

It is ten to one the experiment will convince you that the first essential accessory for good cine work is a tripod.

The two things to look for in a tripod are rigidity and portability. Unfortunately it is difficult to get both, so you may have to decide between a heavy tripod that is really firm, or a light one that needs to be used with care. If weight and bulk are not serious disadvantages, choose the heavy one. A flimsy

Fig. 34. The geared panning movement of the M.P.P. tripod can be very useful to an experienced worker, but it is apt to serve as a temptation to the beginner to pan too frequently.

affair of thin metal tubes that will sway in the wind is worse than useless.

You can get a good tripod for less than ten pounds, or you can pick up a 'disposal' model, wonderfully firm but heavy, for a great deal less. A pan-tilt head to fit it may be bought for perhaps 30s.

A pan-tilt head is useful, not so much for its primary purpose, which is to move the camera up and down (tilting) or laterally (panning) while shooting, but to enable you to get it into the right position before you start. Without it the business of moving first one leg of the tripod and then another can be very irritating, particularly if you are in a hurry, and may leave you with a sloping horizon or verticals that are not true.

Some tripods have a geared arrangement so that you can pan smoothly and slowly (it must always be done very slowly)

Fig. 35. The greater part of a cine camera is concerned with the transport of the film. Only the section within the rectangle is truly 'camera'.

by turning a handle (fig. 34). This is useful to the man who is doing specialised work, but if you are interested only in family and holiday filming, its presence might be a temptation to overdo panning.

Most beginners pan far too much. It is seldom *really* necessary to pan, except to follow action at fairly short range. A better effect can often be obtained by taking two short shots from different angles instead of one long panning shot.

But if you must pan, always keep the camera still for the first two or three seconds and the last two or three. And avoid 'hosepiping' – that is, purposeless panning first left to right, then right to left, then left to right again.

Some tripods have interchangeable feet, one set shod with rubber and the other ending in spikes. This is an advantage, but it is not safe to assume that the rubber feet will grip on a shiny linoleum floor. As a rule they won't, so some device for locking the legs to prevent slipping is useful. One can be bought

Fig. 36. It is easier to hold the camera steady if you can lean your shoulder against a firm support.

for a few shillings (see fig. 38); or the lino may be covered with a large mat.

There will be occasions when a tripod cannot be used, so it is as well to train oneself to hold the camera as steady as possible without one. The best way to grip the camera will depend partly on its weight and shape and partly on your own personal preference. But always stand with the feet well apart; keep the elbows close to the body; use both hands and press the camera against the cheek-bone; and learn how to depress the starting button without jerking the camera. Do *not* hold the breath while the camera is running, but breathe gently and evenly.

Practise with an empty camera, looking at some fixed object through the viewfinder and judging the steadiness of the image in relation to the edges of the frame.

The part of the camera that takes the picture and must therefore be quite steady is the front inch or so; all the rest is the mechanism for transporting the film (fig. 35).

Fig. 37. Unipod with ball-and-socket head and Sportster-Duo camera in position. The Unipod is a good second best when it is not possible to use a tripod.

It is sometimes useful to support the camera on a fence or the back of a chair, or something of the sort; but be sure the support is firm and that the camera does not sway forwards and backwards. In a club production I once had to use the top of an 8 ft. partition between the public bar and the private bar of an inn, standing on a very rickety chair; but the result was all right.

The hand will be much steadier if it is possible to lean the shoulder against something firm – a wall or the body of a car for example – or to support the elbow, even if it is only on your own knee (fig. 36).

There is a half-way house between the tripod and hand-holding – the unipod (see fig. 37). This is a sort of walking-stick consisting of metal tubes, one sliding inside the other so that it can be extended to eye-level; when the handle is removed, the camera is screwed in its place, either directly on the 'stick' or on a stout ball-and-socket head. The unipod is easier

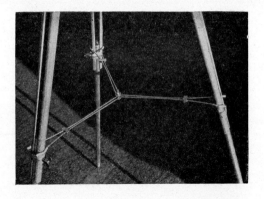

Fig. 38. An adjustable strut, costing a few shillings, may prevent an accident if the foot should be caught against one of the legs of the tripod.

to carry around than a tripod, which is a very real advantage on a holiday, and gives a fair measure of support, particularly if you can manage to wedge it against a fence, or lean your back against a wall.

Other devices include the pistol grip which is available for some cameras and the wrist strap supplied with others. A modification of the unipod is a short rod to which the camera is screwed and which is supported in a sling hung round the neck. Or a loop of stout string may be attached to the camera by means of a screw fitting in the tripod socket; the loop is held down by the foot and pulled taut as the camera is brought to eye level.

These devices are more appropriate to 8 mm. cameras than to the heavier 16 mm. cameras, but it is a mistake to think that a small camera can be held steady more easily than a bigger one without some kind of firm support; and remember that the 8 mm. film is magnified to a greater degree than 16 mm. when projected, so that any unsteadiness will show up more clearly.

You can take chances if you like and shoot off the whole of a holiday film without a tripod or unipod. Thousands do it, but the fact remains that the quality of the film will be vastly improved if you contrive one way or another to use the camera on a firm support.

Fig. 39. In a scene with strong horizontals and verticals it is
important that the camera is really steady.

It has already been hinted that one way to hide camera
wobble is to avoid straight lines, such as the horizon, or the
eaves of a house, or a doorway, parallel to the edges of the
picture. The movement of the straight line up and down on the
screen, or from side to side, is very apparent, particularly if
there is little action in the scene (see fig. 39).

Another dodge is to introduce deliberate movement of the
camera – not level panning from left to right, or straight tilting,
but swinging the camera slowly so that it follows the action.
A child running, for example, would be kept always near the
centre of the picture (fig. 40). This has the added advantage
that you can get nearer to the subject. Instead of taking in a
wide view of the garden, you can include only half or less of
the garden at a time. But if the camera is too near to the subject,
it may be necessary to swing it so quickly that the resulting
picture will be trying to watch.

Camera movement shows up less in brief scenes than in long

Fig. 40. This kind of shot can safely be tackled without a tripod, swinging the camera slowly to follow the child. But the camera should not start to pan for two or three seconds, and it should be still for the last two seconds, letting the child run out of the picture.

ones. If the eye has to adapt itself to a new angle every few seconds, and provided each fresh scene says something a little different from the previous scene, there simply won't be time to notice camera movement unless it is extremely bad. And that is of course a further argument for keeping shots down to an average of about six seconds each.

When a long-focus or telephoto lens is used, a tripod is essential. The purpose of the long-focus lens is to give a bigger image on the screen, and if the image is magnified any movement of the image due to camera wobble will be magnified too.

Chapter 8

FOCUSING

I WAS WATCHING a club film unit at work not long ago. They were shooting a fairly static group at about 25 ft., using a 16 mm. camera and a 1 in. lens. A man measured the distance from camera to group with great precision and said it was 23 ft. 9 in. The cameraman set his lens accordingly and felt sure of correct focus.

Of course the focus would be correct, but even though they were using a big aperture it was quite unnecessary to measure the distance. With the lens set for 25 ft., they could have been sure of everything from $13\frac{1}{2}$ ft. onwards.

The normal lens of a cine camera has great latitude in this matter of 'depth of field' because the focal length of the lens is short. The $\frac{1}{2}$ in. lens of an 8 mm. camera, for example, is so tolerant that cameras are sold with fixed-focus lenses of an aperture of even f/1·9. And many 16 mm. cameras work satisfactorily at f/3·5 and fixed focus.

To be technical for a moment: depth of field varies according to the effective lens diameter; the smaller the diameter of the lens opening, the greater the depth of field. So a $\frac{1}{2}$ in. lens at f/2, and a 1 in. lens at f/4, and a 2 in. lens at f/8, all have the same depth of field, the effective lens diameter being $\frac{1}{4}$ in. in each case.

One reason for the tendency towards lenses of shorter focal length – i.e., 9 or 10 mm. focal length (instead of 12 or 13 mm.) in 8 mm. cameras, and 20 mm. focal length (instead of 25 mm.) in 16 mm. cameras – is that depth of field is thereby increased. Fixed-focus lenses of these shorter focal lengths consequently give a sharp picture over a larger range of distances.

In a fixed-focus camera the lens has been set so that everything from about 6 ft. onwards is tolerably sharp. But at the extremes (i.e. at 6 ft. and also at infinity) definition will be better when a small stop is used than when the lens is at full aperture. For subjects at less than 6 ft., a supplementary lens must be put in front of the normal lens, and then everything will be sharp between about 3½ ft. and 6 ft., or for the distances quoted in the instructions given with the supplementary lens.

The extent to which 'depth of field' can be relied on to give all-over sharpness with a focusing lens is shown in the table

Fig. 41. A measure of this type is useful for distances of up to 6 ft. Beyond that it is seldom necessary to take measurements, or to use a rangefinder, with a normal lens.

on page 141. It will be seen that for distances beyond 6 ft. it should be easy enough to guess; for distances nearer than 6 ft. there is nothing better than one of those steel tape measures that coil up in a little metal case (see fig. 41). Even a length of string with a knot at every foot of its length will be satisfactory.

Measurements should be taken from a point on the camera corresponding to the position of the film in the gate, except when a supplementary lens is used—see page 110; and in the case of a close-up of a face the other end of the tape or string should reach to the cheek.

To measure a distance over 6 ft. it is sufficient to pace it out; but it is as well to practise beforehand so that each pace represents one yard. It is useful, too, to learn to estimate distances; one way, after one has learned to standardize one's paces at one yard, is to stop a few yards from a lamp-post when walking in a quiet street, guess the distance, and count the number of paces it takes to get to it.

If later a long-focus lens is acquired, focusing will have to be more precise. A rangefinder might be used, and some advanced cameras incorporate one; or the rangefinder of a still camera might be employed to read off distances. But the methods suggested above will still be good enough for most scenes, and there is certainly no need for a rangefinder when filming with a normal lens.

There is another way in which a depth-of-field table can be useful. Sometimes it is necessary to film a person against an unattractive background; if the focus is set so that the person is just within the depth of field but the background is not, the figure will stand out better from its surroundings.

The area of sharp focus extends farther beyond the point of critical focus than it extends in front of it. As the table on page 141 shows, if sharpness extends to 15 ft. when the point of critical focus is 10 ft., objects nearer to the camera will be sharp only when they are at least $7\frac{1}{2}$ ft. away. There is a margin of 5 ft. beyond the object focused upon, but a margin of only $2\frac{1}{2}$ ft. in front of that object. It is important to remember this when it is desired to cover a fairly wide area. If, for example, you want to allow for action as near as 10 ft. and as far away as 25 ft., the best point to focus on will be 15 ft.

Figs. 42, 43 and 44. Even without a filter there is usually some indication of cloud in a long shot but with a X2 yellow filter (lens opened up one stop) the clouds will be clearer, and X4 orange filter (lens opened up two stops) will make the sky more dramatic and the distance more distinct.

Chapter 9

FILTERS

(Black-and-white film)

ALL REVERSAL FILM is panchromatic; that is, it is sensitive to all colours; but black-and-white film is more sensitive than the human eye to blue, and somewhat less sensitive to green. So blue tends to photograph too light and green too dark.

This tendency can be corrected by putting in front of the lens (or behind it) a piece of glass or gelatine of suitable colour. But when this is done it is necessary to increase exposure by using a larger aperture.

A colour filter passes freely colours similar to its own, and holds back colours that are opposed to it. For example, a yellow filter has no effect on yellow, but holds back blue; orange and green and red will also hold back blue. Conversely a blue filter would hold back yellow and red if this were desired, e.g. in artificial light (see page 141).

The practical application of this for everyday filming in monochrome is that when the sky is included in a picture, a yellow or yellowish-green or orange filter will make the blue of the sky appear darker and so emphasize the clouds. But in a long shot without a heavy foreground a cloudy sky will seldom appear quite empty (see figs. 42, 43 and 44).

An average yellow or yellow-green filter, described as a 'X2' or 'two times' filter, requires an increase in exposure of one stop. An orange filter is stronger and may require a increase of two stops ('X4'). This would be useful if, for instance, it were desired to film a freckled child and subdue the freckles. A red filter, requiring an increase of three stops, will often make a blue sky appear black.

There are filters specially made to cut down the value of the light reaching the film without affecting the tones of the subject. These are termed 'neutral density' filters and have factors of X2 and X4; i.e. they require the lens to be opened up one stop or two stops. They are useful if the exposure meter or table says f/22 and the smallest aperture on the camera is f/16.

It will be gathered from this that for the great majority of subjects it is not necessary to use a filter. Shots of people doing things seldom need to be filtered; and even when the sky occupies a considerable area of the picture space most people prefer a gentle suggestion of clouds rather than dramatic over-emphasis.

Fig. 45. To cut a piece of gelatine to the required size, fold it in a piece of smooth paper and cut paper and filter together.

It is fun experimenting, but it is best to start modestly by buying a filter in gelatine form such as a piece of Ilford 'Beta', which costs a few pence, rather than spend a lot of money on glass filters which may never be used. With most cameras it is easy to fit a circle of gelatine filter in front of or behind the lens. Often it can be dropped into position, or it may be held in place by means of tiny bits of adhesive tape.

Fig. 46. For a scene like this a light yellow filter (with an increase of half a stop) will give a good rendering of clouds and brighten the tones of the foliage.

To cut the gelatine, the surface of which must never be touched by the fingers, a circle of the correct size to fit the lens should first be drawn on a piece of stout, smooth paper. The paper should then be folded, the gelatine placed in the fold, and paper and filter cut together (see fig. 45). A circle drawn round a sixpence is often just right.

The Beta filter, which is yellowish-green, is 'X2' and therefore requires an increase in exposure of one stop. Another Ilford filter, also obtainable in gelatine form, is the Alpha, light yellow and requiring an increase of half a stop. This is often quite good enough (see fig. 46).

If it is decided, however, to start with a glass filter, it is best to get one of yellow-green or yellow with an X2 factor – i.e. requiring an increase of exposure of one stop, such as f/8 instead

Fig. 47. Clouds are not important in a busy scene such as this, where attention is held by movement in the foreground. Still, if there are clouds in the sky, there will usually be some indication of them in a long shot, even without a filter.

of f/11. Filters are specially made to fit most cameras and usually cost something like £1 each.

Glass filters are sometimes made of dyed glass, or they may consist of a piece of coloured gelatine sandwiched between two pieces of glass. In either case the glass will be of high quality, and the filter must be handled with the same care as a lens. Scratches or dirt on the filter will have the same effect on the picture as a messy lens.

When a filter is used in front of a lens, it should be protected from stray light by a lenshood. Many cameras incorporate a lenshood; if this is the case, and if the filter can be put between the lens and the hood, that is all right. If the camera has no lenshood one should certainly be bought – or made – to give

74

Fig. 50. For most purposes a happy mean will be found in a X2 yellow or yellow-green filter (open up one stop).

maximum protection without cutting off the picture at the corners. A short tube of stiff black paper is better than nothing. It serves not merely to shield the lens, or filter, from direct sunlight – which would fog the film – but from the reflected light of bright objects just outside the field of view. The sea, for example, or a whitish promenade, which may throw sufficient light upwards to cause trouble.

For filters to be used with colour film, see page 78.

Opposite: *Fig. 48 (top).* A light yellow filter (with an increase of half a stop) will bring clouds out clearly, but without emphasis. *Fig. 49 (bottom).* A X4 orange filter (lens opened up two stops) will make the sky more dramatic.

Chapter 10

COLOUR

MOST FILMING with 8 mm. cameras is done in colour, and it undoubtedly makes family films more attractive than black-and-white. Colour brings back the scene so much more vividly; it proves beyond dispute that little Jenny's hair really was golden when she was three, not the ambiguous tint suggested by monochrome; and flowers and foliage and skies look real.

In America Kodak no longer market 8 mm. monochrome film; in this country they do, but it costs the same as Kodachrome. Anyhow, we see enough black-and-white on the TV screen.

Black-and-white is used more often on 16 mm. The wider gauge is better for subjects where fine detail is important and where colour doesn't matter so much. In particular, indoor filming is much easier in monochrome, and if a documentary film includes a number of interior scenes, black-and-white may be desirable. But for outdoor filming on 16 mm. colour film is the usual choice, despite its higher cost.

There are a few things to remember when using colour film:

(1) It is slower than black-and-white film. Kodachrome for daylight use is rated at ASA 10, whereas Panatomic X 8 mm. black-and-white film is ASA 25 – a little more than twice as fast. Kodak Plus X (16 mm.) is ASA 50; and the very fast Tri-X is ASA 200, twenty times as fast as Kodachrome.

(2) Colour film has little latitude, which means that it is very important to use the correct aperture when filming. An error of half a stop can be tolerated, but not more. However as the film is normally used in sunlight, and the instructions given with the film are clear, this should cause little trouble. F/8 at 16 f.p.s. in sunlight will take care of most subjects on Kodachrome.

(3) As there is little latitude, it follows that subjects with

strong lighting contrasts are not as satisfactory as those with flat lighting. The best lighting for colour is soft diffused sunshine on a day when the sun is making its way through slight haze; it makes all contrasts of high-lights and shadows gentler without spoiling contrasts of tone between one colour and another. And, by the way, do not believe anyone who tells you *never* to use colour film for against-the-light shots. Try it some time, on a day of hazy sunshine, with a scene in medium distance. Colours will be diffused and detail suppressed, but there will be a glow of light over the whole picture that will make it well worth while.

(4) Colour film requires that the light shall be of the right kind. Film made for use in daylight cannot be used in artificial light, and film made for use with photofloods cannot be used in daylight, unless a compensating filter is employed (see (6) below); it cannot even be used satisfactorily with the light of ordinary household lamps because these have a lower colour temperature, i.e., the light has an orange tinge as compared with the light of photofloods.

The film will record variations in lighting that may not be noticed when looking at the scene. For example, on a day with a blue sky a wet road will appear deep blue, because it reflects the blue of the sky. And if a person is wearing a yellow scarf, or standing close to a red wall, the colour of the scarf or wall will be seen reflected in the flesh tones of the face. You can observe these things with the eye if you look for them, and train yourself to do so, but it is only too easy to overlook them.

I have a shot of a pretty baby in a white frock, turned terracotta by the light reflected from the wall of a house. In early morning or late afternoon a scene may have an overall golden or reddish tone, perfectly truthful, but sometimes surprising when screened unless there is something in the film to denote the time of day.

(5) Not all colour film is of the same speed, so after using Kodachrome, Gevacolor or Ferraniacolor, all of which are rated at ASA 10, be sure to read the instructions before changing to Agfacolor (ASA 16) or Anscocolor (ASA 20) and make due allowance for the faster emulsion.

(6) With colour film a filter is, generally speaking, unneces sary, except when film intended for artificial light is used in day light. There is a wide range of filters designed to correct the varying colour values of daylight, but these are for the expert and for amateur work the rendering of daylight scenes on film designed for use in daylight will usually be found quite satis factory without any filter at all.

A 'haze' filter may, however, be used with daylight colour film when the light is blueish, e.g. at the seaside with a blue sky. The haze filter appears colourless, and it does not require any increase in exposure, but it cuts down the effect of the ultra-violet light to which the film, but not the human eye, is sensitive. Generally speaking it gives a sort of mellowness to the picture.

When colour film made for use in artificial light is used in daylight, a filter is essential. Artificial light is relatively deficient in blue, so film for use in artificial light is more sensitive to blue than daylight film. When it is used in daylight, a filter must be employed to cut down the blue content of daylight. For Kodachrome A the appropriate filter is Wratten 85, which can be bought in gelatine form. Kodachrome A with the Wratten 85 filter is the same speed as daylight Kodachrome.

Daylight Kodachrome can be used in photoflood light with a suitable blue filter (Wratten 80 B) but this cuts down the speed of the film so much that it is much better to employ the film made specially for artificial light.

(7) Beginners often make the mistake of crowding too much colour into a scene, but a film which contains a succession of vivid reds, greens, yellows and blues will look garish and tawdry. It is more effective to use brilliant colours sparingly. For example, in a landscape scene which has no strong colour contrasts, the figure of a child in a red frock, in middle dis tance, will provide an agreeable accent; a lot of children in bright clothing of various hues would make a muddle of things, for the eye would be attracted first here and then there. A restricted use of strong colour makes for concentration of interest; a flood of colour is distracting.

Chapter 11

SCENES AND SEQUENCES

AS INDIVIDUAL SHOTS are best kept short, it follows that when we want to film an incident that cannot be portrayed in a few seconds, it must be built up by linking together several shots (i.e. 'scenes') into a 'sequence'.

Let us suppose we want to include in our family film a record of a visit to the children by Uncle Bob. We could of course set the camera up in advance near the front door, start to shoot as Bob enters the gate, and fire off a few feet of film as he walks up the path. If a tripod were used the picture would be dead steady; but it would probably be deadly dull too. One continuous shot would be too lengthy, and so tend to become wearisome; yet if Bob's visits were rare, even twenty seconds would be scanty time to devote to the occasion. Moreover, if Bob were not expecting to be filmed, it is possible the shot would not show him at his best.

An alternative approach would be to stand five or six feet to the side of the path and swing the camera slowly so that it followed Bob's progress, cutting at a point when Bob was near enough to appear on the screen in close-up. This could be done without a tripod, for the slow panning of the camera, with interest centred on the figure, would conceal any wobble. But it would not be much better than the first method.

A more interesting way of recording the incident would be to stage the whole thing. It would not all be done at the actual moment of Bob's arrival, and it would require a little forethought and arranging of things. But it is a common-place that the best 'spontaneous' snapshots and film shots are arranged. In cine it is more important that a thing shall look right than that it should be a faithful record of what actually occurred. You wouldn't take a photograph of a group of people without arranging them so that they all showed up to good advantage. Similarly there is no virtue in filming something 'just as it happened' if it will look better, and indeed truer, with a little stage management.

So *before* Bob comes we take:

(1) the hostess (Bob's sister) opening the door of the house from within, and waving her hand;
(2) the children running round a corner of the house.

At the actual time of arrival we take:

(3) a short shot of Bob just after he enters the gate and starts to walk up the path;
(4) Bob, with the children hanging on, greeting his sister.

The rest is re-enacted half an hour later, and as Bob has by now got used to the idea of being filmed, he will readily join in the fun. So we take:

(5) a fairly distant shot of the garden gate; Bob comes to it and has slight difficulty with the latch;
(6) the same, but closer; Bob looks up, giving a clear picture of his face, waves his hand and opens the gate;
(7) the children meet him half-way up the path and seize his hands, or snatch presents he has brought for them.

After processing these scenes would be cut up and rejoined in the order:

$$5-1-6-2-3-7-4.$$

Scenes 5 and 4 should occupy about six seconds each; the other scenes three or four seconds each, the total screen time being thirty seconds.

The sequence would then appear thus; Bob comes to the gate and has difficulty with the latch; his sister waves to him; Bob waves back and succeeds in opening the gate; the children start to run round the corner of the house to meet him; Bob begins to walk up the path; the children meet him; with the children hanging on, he greets his sister.

80

Fig. 51. In this kind of medium shot there is room for action without varying the position of the camera, but a few close-ups like fig. 52 will help enliven the film.

It is a bit more trouble to film the incident like this instead of firing off the camera on the spur of the moment, but it is much more fun and well worth the trouble. Set down in words it may seem over elaborate, but the sequence will look quite natural when projected, it will give clear portraits of everyone concerned, and convey faithfully the atmosphere of the visit.

A film will always look better if it is built up from sequences instead of being merely a collection – and possibly a jumble – of single shots. Within the sequence each scene must be related to the one that precedes it and to the one that follows, and all must have a direct bearing on the theme of the sequence – Bob's visit in the example given – even though it might be convenient to shoot an odd scene (to fill in a gap) days or weeks after the other shots were taken.

In making notes to be used when filming (technically, preparing a shooting script) it is convenient to decide the scale on which the subject is to be presented; whether a person is to be shown in close-up, medium shot or long shot, for example. Symbols such as C.U., M.S., L.S. and so on are used, and the thing to remember about them is that they are quite relative. A long shot of an elephant might be taken at 200 ft.; a long shot of a fly at 1 ft.

A C.U. is a shot in which the subject (head and shoulders in the case of a person) pretty well fills the frame. A big close-up (B.C.U.) will include only the face, or part of it, such as the eyes and mouth. In a L.S. of a person the figure will be quite small. A M.S. is something between the two.

C.M.S. (close medium shot), M.L.S. (medium long shot), M.C.U. (medium close-up) are variations of the medium shot.

The important thing is that variety in camera position makes for interest. A succession of scenes all taken at 15 or 20 ft. can be rather dull. So when filming it is wise to take plenty of shots at 4 ft. and 6 ft. and mix them in with the medium shots and an odd long shot (figs. 51 and 52).

Fig. 52.

The angle of approach should be varied too; it is a mistake to take everything from directly in front of the subject. Variety may be introduced into the middle of a bit of action by stepping two or three paces to the left, or to the right, or by moving until the camera is at right angles to the position previously held. Sometimes, but not too often, an interesting effect may be obtained by using the camera low down, possibly even at ground level, shooting upwards; or by shooting down from an upstairs window.

Chapter 12

LIGHTING OUT OF DOORS

LISTENING to a lecture by a man who makes his living by taking photographs to illustrate books and magazines and so on, I was struck by the number of times he said: 'When I came on this subject the light wasn't right, so I had to come back the next day before the sun got so far round.'

The choice of the best kind of lighting is more important to the still photographer than to the cine man because his picture will rely to a greater extent for its appeal on good contrasts and pleasing patterns of light and shade. In cine the thing that attracts and pleases the eye is the movement of the people or things in front of the camera. If their actions are completely absorbing, no one is likely to notice whether the lighting was as good as it might have been.

This fact can be very consoling if you ever want to make a scripted film which cannot be shot all at the same time. You may be acutely conscious that the first part of the action is filmed on a clear sunny day, whereas the second part has to be taken when the sky is overcast and there are no shadows. But if the action grips the attention and a good proportion of the scenes are shot at fairly close quarters, it is unlikely that the difference will be noticed by the audience – unless, of course, they are deliberately critical. This is true even with colour film, although when the sun is obscured colour values do change, and lack of 'colour continuity' is a thing to be avoided whenever possible.

After all, if we meet a friend in the street, we recognize him by his features, figure, habit of walking, clothing perhaps; as likely as not we do not notice whether the lighting on his face is from the front, or the side, or from behind him. We

Fig. 53. An example of back lighting. Note the characteristic outlining of the figures in light, and the way this is helped by the dark background.

may not even notice whether he is in the sun or in the shade.

But while lighting is less important than subject-matter or action, the arrangement of a scene, or a person, or a group of people, so that the direction of the light and its intensity are the most suitable, may make all the difference between an effective picture and a poor one And the first essential is to learn to recognize what is the most suitable lighting for filming.

We have to learn to see as the camera sees, and to appreciate that the camera is less tolerant than the eye to differences between light tones and dark tones.

When filming in colour, contrasts between one tint and another exert the same sort of pull as contrasts of light and shade in monochrome. You don't want both kinds of contrast in the same scene, which is one of the reasons why you are advised to use flat lighting for colour work. But there are times

Fig. 54. Side lighting with a low sun.

Fig. 55. The sun was shining directly towards the camera. The lenshood might not have been adequate, so the camera was placed in a patch of shade under an overhanging tree.

Fig. 56. A semi-silhouette effect, obtained by shooting directly into the light, can be very effective and contrasts well with scenes that have more conventional lighting.

when there is little colour contrast in a subject, and then dramatic lighting contrast may be effective. A close-up in strong sunshine of a person in clothing of nondescript colour is an example; in the result there will be so little noticeable colour that the portrait will be almost in monochrome, so the type of lighting appropriate to monochrome is acceptable – up to a point. And the *point* is that as colour film has less latitude than black-and-white film, the contrasts will appear greater.

Out of doors the lighting is always, or almost always, directional; that is, it is stronger in front, or at the side, or behind the subject than it is in other directions. This is obvious if the sun is shining, but even on a dull day one part of the sky will be brighter than the rest, and that will provide the main source of light.

Fig. 57. Side lighting with hazy sunshine. The dark background was appropriate for the shot.

If we film someone on a dull day with his back to the bright part of the sky, the face will be dark and modelling poor. So on a dull day it is better to shoot with the subject pretty well facing the brightest part of the sky. It is no good trying to get a sunny effect when the sun isn't shining; but provided there is interest in the scene, and sufficient action to hold the attention, the rather flat lighting may not matter, even in black-and-white.

When the sun is shining, the best arrangement for black-and-white filming, unless some special effect is desired, is to point the camera so that the sun is neither directly behind the camera nor exactly to one side, but somewhere in between these two positions. Frontal sunshine – that is, with the sun behind the camera – causes screwed-up eyes and gives a rather flat picture without interesting shadows.

Lighting from the side can be dramatic and intriguing, but

Fig. 58. There are no dark shadows under the eyes because light was reflected up by the sand. In a garden a white cloth or newspaper would serve similarly as a reflector.

with close-ups in strong sunshine one side of the face will be much brighter than the other. It will usually be necessary to relieve the shadows by using a reflector.

Back lighting – that is, with the sun behind the *subject* – can be very attractive if a glamorous picture is desired rather than one with a lot of detail. A few shots of this kind make for variety in a record which is mainly straightforward filming 'with the light'. A dark background will add to the effect and emphasize the characteristic rim of light around the subject. If the background is not subdued, this effect may be lost in a muddle of light tones and dark tones.

The sky should never be included in scenes taken against the light; it will simply come out white, or pink on colour film. Filters will not help.

Fig. 59. Here again the white roadway has given adequate relief to the shadows, but frontal sunshine has caused screwed-up eyes.

Whatever the direction of the light, there are two additional factors that will modify the result. The first is the height of the sun in the heavens. If it is near the zenith, strong shadows will be thrown downwards, making eyes appear as caverns. If it is low in the sky, early or late in the day, shadows will be less intense, but they will be longer and may make attractive patterns. The lens must be carefully shielded when the sun is low; if the regular lenshood is inadequate, an umbrella, or something of the sort, may be held so that it casts a shadow on the camera. With the camera on a tripod the cameraman may be able to hold a hat or a book just outside the field of view of the lens.

The second modifying factor is reflection. Light may be deliberately reflected into the shadows on a face, for example, by something white held 3 or 4 ft. away. A towel or a newspaper would do, but it should not be too close to the subject. A white wall not far away will serve as a reflector; a dark wall on the other hand will cut off any light from that direction.

A sandy beach or seaside promenade will reflect a lot of light; and shadows will always be softer on a day with white clouds than when the sky is uniformly blue, because the clouds act as reflectors of the sunlight. On the other hand when there is a deep blue sky reflected by a lot of water, the whole scene may acquire a too-blue tinge on colour film unless a haze filter is used as a corrective.

The instructions enclosed with colour film explain the use of the haze filter in these circumstances, and at high altitudes. Always read these instructions carefully; the information in them is important although it may be compressed into few words. And never take an unfamiliar type of film away on a holiday without trying out a length first.

Chapter 13

LIGHTING INDOORS

SIMPLE indoor filming in black-and-white at children's parties, family get-togethers or small amateur dramatic shows is almost as easy as filming out of doors. With two small photofloods in reflectors, which can be easily made at home, close-ups in a room with light walls can be filmed on medium-speed film at f/4, and medium shots at f/2·8; or these apertures may be reduced to f/6·3 and f/4·5 respectively by using a faster film. Even with one lamp acceptable results are possible; but two lamps are decidedly better.

Indoor filming in colour isn't so easy because, as colour film is slower than black-and-white, it requires a lot more light. Moreover, while you can safely mix artificial light and daylight when filming in black-and-white, you would get unsatisfactory results if you tried to do this with colour film; using type-A film, the parts of the subject lit from the windows would be too blue; and using daylight -type film, the parts lit by artificial light would be too yellow. The only way round this would be to fit blue filters on the photofloods, or amber-coloured translucent screens to the windows, and that would involve more trouble than most of us are prepared to take.

However, if you don't mind using a lot of photofloods, you can film indoor scenes in colour, and the following instructions apply as with black-and-white. Whatever film is used, exposure should be calculated with the aid of an exposure meter or based on the instructions given with the film. Note that Kodachrome A is rated at ASA 16 when used with photoflood lighting, although when used in daylight with a Wratten 85 filter it is the same speed as daylight Kodachrome, i.e., ASA 10.

The small photofloods, which cost 2s. 6d. each, consume

275 watts each, so two or even three may be run off a lighting circuit. But because they are overrun, the light output of each lamp is equivalent to 800 watts.

They get very hot and the average life of a lamp is two hours. But a lot of filming can be done in two hours, and the lamps need be left full on only while the camera is running. The lamps seem extremely bright in comparison with ordinary room lighting, but in relation to daylight out of doors they are not really powerful.

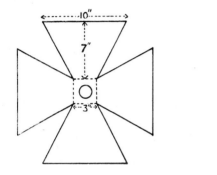

Fig. 60. An efficient reflector for a photoflood lamp can be made from thin white card and mounted on a stand of wood or stout wire.

The lamps have bayonet fittings, like a domestic lamp, and can be used in ordinary lamp sockets; but they are much more efficient in reflectors, not only because the value of the light is increased several times over, but because the reflector diffuses it. A naked lamp will throw hard shadows, but in a reflector the same lamp will give a softer illumination.

Metal reflectors can be bought with tubular stands and ball-and-socket heads, or with supports that will stand on a table or clip to the back of a chair. These cost from a few shillings for the simpler types to a few pounds for the more elaborate ones. But it is an easy matter to make a reflector of thin white card, and this can be very nearly as good as the commercial article for black-and-white filming. But for colour film, when you will need all the light you can get, metal reflectors should be used.

The working life of the lamps will be lengthened if they are used with a series-parallel switch. This not only reduces the length of time they are burning at full strength but – what is more important – avoids damage from the surge of current when they are switched fully on from cold.

The two lamps are first switched on in series, giving a relatively dim light which is nevertheless good enough for focusing and arranging the scene; they are switched fully on during actual filming. A wiring diagram of a series-parallel switch is given on page 142. There are other methods of arranging this safeguard; the switch from an old electric cooker, for example, can be used quite satisfactorily.

However, a series-parallel switch is not essential. Without it one may have to buy an extra lamp or two a year, which is not a serious matter. And if a photoflood lamp burns out after only five minutes, as sometimes happens, it is quite likely that the next lamp may last for many months.

An alternative, or additional, means of economizing is to use lamps rated at a higher voltage than the actual supply, e.g. 230 volt lamps on 210 volt mains. The difference in light output is very small; but lamps used in this way would not be suitable for use with colour film.

Arranging the lamps to give best results is more of a problem in an ordinary room than it would be in, say, a studio, because it is not always possible to find space for a lamp just where it ought to be put for best effect. But a small room with light walls has the advantage that the walls serve to some extent as reflectors; this might make a difference of about half a stop, and, more important, it will soften the lighting. But when using colour film beware of coloured walls which might give a false colour cast to the scene.

It was mentioned that out-of-doors the light is almost always directional – there is one main source of light – and the things to be considered for effective filming are whether the light falls on the subject from the front or the side or the rear; whether the light is high or low in relation to the subject; and whether the light is modified by reflection.

Exactly the same considerations apply to filming with photofloods. If the lighting is to look natural, the best course is to imitate as far as possible outdoor conditions by using one lamp (or possibly a pair or group of lamps) as the main source of light, and to arrange this so that it gives a pleasing effect; a second lamp should then be used to 'fill in' the shadows and soften the directional strength of the main lamp, just as is done out of doors by the use of reflectors, natural or artificial.

The second lamp must be less powerful than the main lamp, or it would kill the shadows, so it should be placed farther away from the subject. As the intensity of light varies inversely as the square of the distance it travels, a lamp at 6 ft. from the subject will give only one-quarter the light given by a lamp at 3 ft. – not one-half. And in cine a ratio of 2:1 is usually considered about right as between main lamp and fill-in. So when the main lamp is 3 ft. from the subject, the fill-in lamp will normally be at 4½ ft.; if the main lamp is 4 ft. from the subject, the fill-in will be at 6 ft.

A third lamp behind the sitter, and fairly high up, might be used to put a gleam on the hair; or alternatively it could be employed to liven up the background. But 'effects' lighting of this kind is not really necessary in home filming, and the lamps will not help exposure. That is to say, they must not be taken into account in calculating the aperture to be used, and must be switched off while an exposure meter reading is taken.

Fig. 61 shows a simple arrangement of two (or three) photofloods for home filming. To give good modelling the main lamp (A) is placed to one side and about 2 ft. higher than the sitter's face; it could of course be on the other side, over by the far wall, if desired. The fill-in lamp (B) is as near to the camera as possible, so that while it will cast no shadows itself, it will add something to both the light and dark features. The distance between the fill-in lamp and the sitter will be

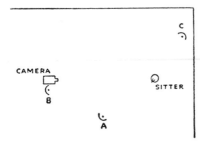

Fig. 61. A simple arrangement of two (or three) No. 1 photofloods for a C.U. in an ordinary room. A is the main lamp, 4 ft. from the sitter and 6 ft. high. B is the fill-in lamp, as close to the camera as possible and at camera level, 6 ft. from the sitter. C, which is optional, is behind the sitter as high as is practicable, shining down on the hair from approximately 4 ft.

half as much again as the distance between the main lamp and the sitter.

The third lamp (c), if one is used, is high and to the side-rear, about the same distance from the sitter's head as (a). It will not affect the camera stop to be used, and care must be taken that it does not shine into the camera lens.

There are of course many other arrangements of two or three lamps that would give satisfactory and interesting results, and it is fun experimenting. But it is essential that, first, there should be one predominating light; second, the position of this light should be decided in relation to the sitter, not in relation to the camera, and it should usually be higher than the sitter's face; third, the second lamp (the 'fill-in') must be farther away from the sitter than the main lamp, and placed so that it does not introduce any fresh shadows. Ideally its position should coincide with that of the camera, or be in the line camera-to-sitter, and at camera level; as this is impossible, it is best to put it slightly to one side, on the same side of the camera as the main lamp.

The above advice applies in the main to black-and-white filming; with colour, as we do not want marked contrasts of light and shade, there should be less difference between the lamp-to-subject distance for the main lamp and for the fill-in lamp. And of course as colour film is slower than black-and-white film, you will need more lamps, or the more powerful No. 2 photofloods instead of No. 1 photofloods. You can if

Fig. 62. For this kind of party scene it may be impossible to put lamps just where you would like them, and trailing lengths of flex might be dangerous. It is best to fix lamps on the picture rail and hold the camera in the hand.

you like put all lamps as close as possible to the camera, or in line with the camera. This will give flat lighting, which wouldn't be very satisfactory with black-and-white, but is quite suitable when you are relying on colour to provide contrasts.

The word 'sitter' has been used rather freely because the lighting scheme is particularly suitable for a close-up or medium close-up of one person. But it will suit a group of two or three people quite well. A risk to be avoided is that one person may cast a shadow on another.

When filming several people who may move about the room, as at a children's party, arrangements may have to be somewhat makeshift. It is unwise, and may be dangerous, to clutter up the floor with lamp-stands and lengths of flex. The best

97

plan will probably be to fix as many photofloods as are available round the picture rail, pointing generally in the same direction as the camera; other photofloods may be put in place of the usual room lights, and one lamp kept close to the camera, if this is possible. It is very much a case of hoping for the best, but if there is plenty of activity no one will bother about double shadows on some of the faces, or about an underlit background. The great thing is to put enough light where it is wanted so as to be able to use a fairly small stop and get good depth of field.

Here are a few points to watch when filming with photofloods:

1. When using black-and-white film, but not with colour film, the ordinary room lighting should be kept full on; it will not affect the aperture to be used, but it will make the glare of the photofloods less dazzling to the eyes.

2. The main or modelling lamp (lamp A in fig. 61) should be switched on first, by itself. It will cast very heavy shadows. These should be studied, particularly the shadow of the nose. A slight movement of the lamp to one side, or up or down, may suggest an improvement. When the light of the fill-in lamp is added, everything will be so bright that the shadows will hardly be visible; but the camera will see them.

3. Reflections from spectacles or bright objects within the field of view can be troublesome. A slight raising or lowering of the head, or small adjustment of one of the lamps, should overcome the spectacles difficulty. Other reflecting object may have to be moved, or the camera position changed.

4. The background should not be too assertive, and a sitter should not be placed so close to a wall that unwanted shadow fall on it.

5. A tripod is very desirable, particularly for close-ups but for party scenes with plenty of movement the camera can be hand-held.

6. The lens of the camera should normally be on a level with the eyes of the sitter when filming in close-up, even though this may involve lying flat on the floor for pictures of a small child.

7. Light clothing is to be preferred to dark.

8. As filming will usually be at a big aperture, focusing must be accurate.

9. It is just as well to know where the fuse box is and to have fuse wire ready to hand in case of mishap.

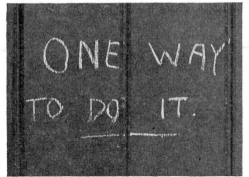

Fig. 63. A simple and efficient form of titling—words written in chalk on a door or wall. In this case the door might open slowly to reveal one of the characters in the film.

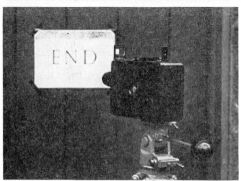

Fig. 64. Another easy way to make a title: a hand-drawn card affixed to a door and filmed in the open.

Fig. 65. With strong side lighting from a single photoflood, felt letters on a pale blue background stand out against their shadows.

Chapter 14

TITLES

NO MATTER how simple the theme, a film should always have a main title. If it is a record of a journey, or of several incidents not obviously connected, it may need a few sub-titles as well. And for the convenience of both projectionist and audience, the screen should give warning when the reel is coming to an end.

The purpose of the main title is to identify the film, and for a family record a word or two will often be sufficient, such as 'Family Album', or 'Cornwall', and the year. Dating the film may seem unnecessary at the time, but it will avoid confusion when half a dozen 'family albums' have been compiled.

Sub-titles should be similarly factual, using the smallest possible number of short words. It is bad, for example, to say, 'When she attained the age of fourteen months, Susan ventured a few steps unaided', because it can be said better in half the number of words: 'At fourteen months – all by herself.' Instead of, 'We drew up for refreshment in a picturesque spot near Selworthy', it is quite enough to say, 'Near Selworthy', and let the picture tell the rest. 'Exhausted, we took time off for a breather', can be expressed just as well in the one word: 'Whew!'

The final sub-title should consist simply of the words, 'The End'; or, if you want to be a trifle different, 'End'. Nothing is gained by striving after originality with a phrase such as: 'That's all for now, folks.'

The main title should run for ten or twelve seconds; this will give the audience time to break off any conversation, and the projectionist an opportunity to adjust focus, if he wants to. For sub-titles one second should be allowed as a rule for every two words, with a minimum of two seconds; unusual words require a bit longer, but a sub-title with a dozen quite short words might last only four seconds. Titles that stay on the screen too long can be irritating.

Credit titles are unnecessary in a film that is to be shown only to friends, and even if it is hoped to show it to a wider public, a succession of announcements saying who produced, scripted, directed, edited, titled, and so on may look a bit silly. If for some reason this information is desirable, it is best to put it at the end of the film and as concisely as possible.

When titles are made only occasionally, it may seem extravagant to spend a lot of money on a titler, and not worth the trouble of making one for oneself. But unless you are sure you are only going to be a casual filmer, you can assume that you will need one sooner or later. It is nice to have a piece of really good apparatus, and of course a titler is very convenient in use.

Amateur cine societies sometimes keep apparatus of this kind for the use of their members; or a member who possesses it may be willing to lend it to others. But it is not difficult to make titles without a titler.

A rough-and-ready method is to write the title in chalk on a fence or blackboard or door, and simply film it as you would film anything else (see fig. 63). Or the title can be drawn or painted or printed on a card which is stuck up on a door and filmed (see fig. 64). Place names can be shots of road or railway station signs. But in all cases the camera must be level with the central point of the title and a tripod should be used. A title made with a hand-held camera is always unsatisfactory.

It is possible to make titles by filming typewritten captions at a distance of about 18 in. if the lens will focus down to that distance or if a suitable supplementary lens is available. But typescript always looks what it is, and the too regular spacing of the letters appears awkward on the screen.

A more professional appearance can be got by using sets of letters sold specially for cine titling; there are several varieties of metal, plastic, wood and felt. Some metal letters are magnetized and stay put when the metallic background is erected vertically. Some plastic letters are self-adhesive and may be detached from their support for further use.

The cheapest letters are those made of felt; a few shillings

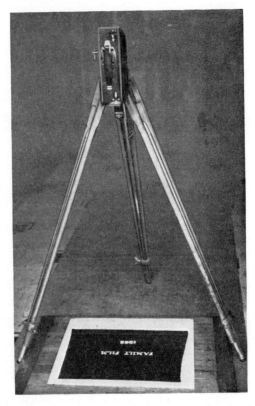

Fig. 66. Titling by daylight indoors, near open French windows. The title card is 27 in. from the plane of the film in the camera.

will buy enough to make quite a long title. They are $\frac{3}{8}$ in. or $\frac{1}{2}$ in. high and are used on a background of felt or similar material. They can, of course, be used over and over again if they are handled with care; tweezers should be used to pick them up, not the fingers.

Black background cards sold for use with felt letters usually measure 8 in. × 6 in., which is rather too small for convenience. Even if the card is framed precisely so that the whole area is used, the letters will appear too large on the screen; and for some purposes it is better to use a background that is not dead black.

Fig. 67. The Presgrip titler has a cast frame and provision for title screens up to a width of 14 in.

Pieces of thin felt can be bought quite cheaply from an art needlework shop and when stuck on card (using rubber mountant) are quite suitable. Dark green felt is best for most plain titles, and is good with colour film; a red background nearly always looks wrong in colour. Pale blue is useful if it is desired to show texture in the background, or to let the letters throw shadows (see fig. 65). Black felt is used if the lettering is to be superimposed on a scene.

The pieces of felt measure about 12 in. × 10 in., which allows a generous margin for possible errors. A mask of thin card is placed over the felt while the letters are being arranged, to make sure the title is kept within the limits of the area to be filmed, and a strip of card marked off in inches from the centre helps to get the lettering straight and central.

The approximate areas covered by the normal lens of an 8 mm., 9·5 mm., or 16 mm. camera at different filming distances are shown on page 143. At 27 in. the lettering of felt letters is quite big enough, without being over-assertive.

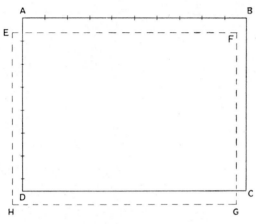

Fig. 68.

The most convenient method of working is to put the title card on the floor (or, rather, on a drawing-board laid on the floor) and the camera on a firm tripod, tilted down at an angle of 90°; but other methods of supporting the camera firmly so that it points directly downwards may suggest themselves. A spirit level laid on the back of the camera may be useful to make sure it is correctly tilted.

It is not always safe to rely on the camera finder to give precise framing of a title. A test with one quite expensive camera showed that when the camera was trained on a rectangle such as ABCD in fig. 68, the area actually filmed was EFGH.

Fig. 69. Frame enlargement of a title made by superimposing white lettering on a background in which the shadows of an overhanging branch sway to and fro.

Fig. 70. This is a simple titling trick. The title card is filmed upside down and a ruler drawn slowly across to wipe away the lettering. When projected the action appears in reverse, the words forming themselves as the ruler moves.

So rectangles like these were drawn on the board on which the title card was to be placed. Rectangle ABCD was made to fill the frame of the finder exactly and then the title card was put down so that the area to be filmed fell correctly over the space EFGH.

This adjustment, needless to say, applied to that particular camera only, and the relative positions of the two rectangles had to be found by experiment.

The best light for titling is daylight, out of doors if it can be managed; indoors, near a french window, open or without curtains, is satisfactory, but a sheet of white card should be used as a reflector to even up the light.

If the sun in shining when filming titles out of doors, the letters will cast little shadows which may be attractive, particularly when the sun is low. A similar effect can be got with artificial light by putting a photoflood or spotlight very low and fairly close to the title; the part of the title nearest to the lamp will be lighter than the rest, but this too may be agreeable.

Exposure is best calculated with a meter. If a reading is taken on a piece of white card placed in the position the title will occupy, the lens should be opened up three stops when using a black or dark green background, or two stops with the pale blue.

It is a convention that the main title and 'The End' shall be faded in and faded out. This is not essential, but it gives a nice finish to the job. Fading-in can be done by starting with the lens at its smallest aperture and slowly opening it to the correct stop while the camera is running; fading-out is the reverse of this.

It is an advantage to have an assistant to vary the aperture, for any movement of the camera would, of course, spoil the result. Alternatively a fading glass may be used. This is a strip of glass with a spattering of black, graduated so that the glass is clear at one end and opaque at the other; the glass is drawn across the lens during the first (or last) two seconds of the exposure. It costs about 5s.

Instead of fading, titles may be 'wiped' in and out by drawing a piece of black card slowly across the lens. But this device can become tedious if it is used too often.

A main title is made more attractive if it is superimposed on a scene related to the subject of the film; but it is a mistake to use a significant scene for this purpose, or one which contains much action. The audience won't be able to read the title and appreciate the picture in detail simultaneously. A long shot with just a little movement is satisfactory, such as a beach with breaking waves, or a landscape with trees moving in the breeze and perhaps a single distant figure; or an all-overish close-up with gentle movement which has, for preference, some relationship to the theme of the film (see fig. 69).

Elaborate superimposed titles with complicated mixes, fades, tracking shots, explosions and other effects are common in professional films, particularly in trailers, and on television. They are made in the processing laboratories when printing the positive film from negatives, or, on television, by using two cameras and ingenious mechanical devices. The amateur using reversal film cannot hope to compete.

The best way to superimpose a title with reversal film is to use the beginning of a spool, shooting the scene that is to be used as a background for about twenty seconds, and underexposing by half a stop. When the rest of the spool has been used, it is rewound in the dark, put back in the camera, and the appropriate footage exposed again on a title consisting of white letters on a black background, with fading in and out.

The background for the lettering must be really dead black. Black cardboard is not dead black and will often reflect enough light to give a slightly fogged effect. It is a good plan to allow the background scene to remain on the screen for a few seconds after the lettering has been faded out.

The camera must be rock steady when filming both the scene and the lettering. The least indication of wobble will spoil the whole thing.

It is not possible to impose black lettering on a light background, such as a sky, by this method; but it can be done even on reversal film if one is prepared to take the trouble. A sheet of clear glass on which the letters have been painted is set up between the camera and the background scene and the two filmed together, the camera being focused, at a small aperture, so that both glass and background are sharp.

Trick titles can be amusing if they are not overdone. When a camera is used upside down and the film projected backwards, action appears in reverse. This is how scenes are taken showing people walking backwards. I know a man who once filmed in this way a negro boy eating a banana – a perfectly revolting scene.

In titling the card instead of the camera can be put upside down. If, then, a ruler is drawn slowly across the lettering of the title while the camera is running the effect on the screen will be of words appearing mysteriously as the ruler moves (see fig. 70).

If the camera permits of single exposures, a heap of letters may similarly be made to jump their way into a sentence. The completed title is put in position for filming upside down, and the letters moved individually a quarter of an inch at a time until they make a pile in the middle of the card, or perhaps move gradually off the edge and out of sight.

When using single exposures it may be necessary to close down half a stop because with many cameras the shutter is open for rather more than the usual 1/32 sec. when single exposures are made.

These tricks would not be very satisfactory, however, with 8 mm. film because in order to keep the sprocket holes on the right side, the film would have to be reversed back to front when splicing it in; this would throw it slightly out of focus when projected and show the picture as though seen in a mirror—right to left instead of left to right. You could arrange lettering right to left in the first place, or film a scene in a mirror, but there would still be the out-of-focus difficulty.

Travelling titles, made by drawing a long length of titled material smoothly in front of the camera, are things you can work out for yourself. It is possible to make use of the domestic mangle. Tracking with the camera, so that the lettering gets bigger and bigger, or smaller and smaller, needs a horizontal titler and an absolutely smooth track along which the camera is pushed while an assistant adjusts the focus.

Title-making can be quite fascinating, and even the simplest camera (with a supplementary lens if it has fixed focus) can give first-class results and yield a variety of effects. But care must be taken not to get carried away by the fun of it. Too many sub-titles, for example, become wearisome, particularly if they embody wisecracks, witticisms or funny drawings.

When a supplementary lens is used for filming objects at close range, distances must be measured from the front of that lens; at other times measurements should be from the plane of the film in the camera.

Chapter 15

EDITING

SOMETIMES at a cine club a member brings along a reel of holiday film, interesting enough and quite well photographed, but consisting of a number of lengths strung together just as they came back from the processing station. Every now and again there is a flash of perforations, indicating the end of one length or the beginning of another; occasional scenes are so badly overexposed that the glare hurts the eyes; some scenes are so lengthy that one longs for the end, while others are cut off with a jerk because the camera spool ran out unexpectedly.

A film presented in this way shows up very badly in comparison with other films that have been trimmed and pruned a little; for while a holiday or family film seldom needs elaborate treatment, it will always be improved by the process known as editing.

Drastic editing may consist of calculated cross-cutting, with split-second timing of scenes designed to produce dramatic effects. It may involve the scrapping of half or even three-quarters of the film as it came out of the camera, for the inflexible rule is: 'When in doubt, leave it out.'

But that kind of editing demands a lot of time and thought, and costs a lot in wasted film stock. In a straightforward record film it is better to get one's effects, as far as possible, when using the camera. Editing will then amount to no more than rearranging scenes here and there so that the film progresses smoothly from an attractive beginning to a logical finish, cutting out bits that are irrelevant, repetitive or uninteresting, and putting in titles.

Some apparatus is needed: a splicer, a pair of rewind arms,

some film cement, a pair of scissors and an old handkerchief or similar piece of rag. Some arrangement must also be made for sorting lengths of film into order before they are joined together.

A splicer will cost anything from about two to five or six guineas. It is possible to make just as good a join with a cheap splicer as with an expensive one, but it isn't so easy; the more expensive type is quicker in operation and does not require as much manipulative skill.

A splice is made by overlapping the beginning of one length of film with the end of the preceding length to the extent of 3/32 in. and joining them together by means of special film cement. The spliced portion always includes a sprocket hole.

Obviously the back of one piece of film (the shiny side) must be joined to the front (dull side) of the other, and before this is done the emulsion must be scraped from the dull side. Most splicers incorporate a scraper, which may be designed for use dry or after moistening the narrow band of emulsion that is to be scraped away. If no scraper is provided it may be necessary to use the blade of a penknife or a razor blade to scrape the film; in fact it is always useful to have a sharp penknife handy to get an absolutely clean scrape at the edges.

If a scraper is incorporated in the splicer it will usually be made to scrape exactly 3/32 in. of film; if a razor blade or knife is used for the job, there is a risk of scraping just a bit too much, and this will result in a white flash on the screen. Precise scraping – just the right width, and just deep enough to remove the emulsion without damaging and weakening the base – is the mark of a good craftsman.

Rewind arms may be either mounted on a piece of board 2 or 3 ft. long, or made to clamp to the edge of a table. One or both should be geared for rapid winding. When the reels are in position they should be in exactly the same plane; and there should be an effective spring or catch to prevent a reel from falling off the spindle. With ingenuity it is possible to make a satisfactory unit from a couple of geared emery wheels; otherwise it will cost three or four pounds.

Fig. 71. The essentials for splicing are: rewind, splicers, cement and scissors. The white marks on the edge of the board are at 5 in. intervals: the space between two marks therefore represents approximately one second of screen time with 16 mm. or 9·5 mm. film.

The best film cement, it is often said, is that marketed by the makers of the film that is being used, but the 'Universal' varieties sold by Johnsons and May & Baker are satisfactory with most films, including commercially made films. A convenient way to use it is to pour the cement into one of those small bottles with a brush affixed to the screw-cap which originally contain nail varnish; there is nothing better for applying just the right quantity to the scraped film – enough to make a firm joint without any oozing at the edges.

With some splicers it is possible to lift the film after the cement has been applied and wipe the underside with a piece of rag. This makes for a cleaner join, but it must be done quickly, for the cement dries in a few seconds.

When the two ends of the film have been brought together, they must be kept under pressure in the splicer for fifteen to

113

twenty seconds. Then the splice should be examined to see that it is a good one, but no strain should be put on it. The newly spliced film should not be projected for an hour or so.

Sometimes it is difficult to get the joint to stick. If this happens it is a good plan to apply cement to the shiny end as well as to the scraped end. If it is put on the shiny end with a

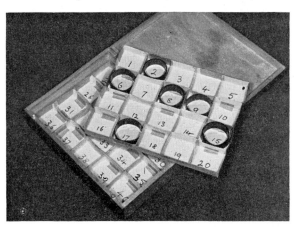

Fig. 72. An editing box of wood or cardboard, with cells about 2 × 2 in., is convenient for sorting together lengths of film after cutting.

quick stroke of the brush and then wiped off immediately with the rag, it will roughen the base and make it adhere more easily.

It is sound practice to start an edited reel with a leader of three or four feet of white waste (i.e. scrap unexposed film) and end the reel with a trailer of two or three feet of black. The title can be written on the white film with an ordinary pen, and the reel will then identify itself and show at a glance whether it has been rewound after projection. White waste can usually be obtained for the asking from a dealer. At the worst it may cost a shilling or two; it is never necessary to spoil good unexposed film in order to make a white leader.

114

Another advantage of the white leader, particularly with 8 mm. film, is that it enables you to see more clearly what you are doing when threading the projector; this may avoid a good deal of exasperation if the light near the projector is poor. (See fig. 79.)

For sorting lengths of film ready for splicing together two devices are convenient. First, a collection of the 50 ft. projection spools on which film comes back after processing, each in its cardboard case and lettered A to Z. These are for fairly long pieces of film. Second, a couple of boxes, about 10 in. × 8 in. × 2 in., each containing two trays divided into compartments, 2 in. × 2 in. × $\frac{3}{4}$ in., and numbered (see fig. 72). Wooden boxes are most suitable, but stout cardboard boxes will do quite well. The trays are made from thin manilla card, the dividing pieces being held in position by bits of gumstrip.

A useful accessory is a viewer, or editor. This is in effect a miniature projector showing a picture some 2 in. × 3 in.; in some models the picture is animated as the film is wound through on to a rewind arm; in others each frame is viewed separately. In either case it is easy to find the point at which the film should be cut to best advantage.

Viewers are rather expensive, but it is often possible to borrow one through a cine club; and in fact, the mechanically minded enthusiast may be able to make one for himself. Failing a viewer the worker who edits only occasionally will find a watchmaker's eyeglass useful, the film being held in front of a sheet of white paper strongly lit, or a piece of opal or ground glass illuminated from behind.

If the film has been scripted before shooting, and each scene numbered by exposing one or two frames on a 'take board', the sorting of shots into sequence should be almost automatic. Almost, but not quite, for there may have been departures from the script, and a few extra scenes may have been put in on the spur of the moment.

Assuming there was no script, the first job, no matter how simple the theme, will be to write one *after* the event. That is to say, a list should be made of the scenes in the order in which they are to be projected – for that is what a script amounts to.

But in order to prepare the script, it will probably be necessary to make a preliminary list of the scenes in the order in which they were *taken*. So as the processed spools are run through the projector, a list of scenes is written down, each scene being given a provisional number: A1, A2, A3, etc., for the first spool; B1, B2, B3, etc., for the next, and so on. At the same time notes are made of anything requiring attention, e.g. 'cut first two seconds'.

When preliminary lists have been made for all the spools that are to be assembled into the reel, a new list will be made of the scenes in the order in which they are to be *shown*. This list, cross-referenced to the preliminary lists, will be the script. It might read like this:

(1) Title;

(2) Mary in garden (A4);

(3) Family comes out of door (A7);

(4) Mary greets grandmother (B13, B14).

'A4' means, of course, the fourth shot on spool A; 'B13 and B14' the thirteenth and fourteenth shots on spool B, and so on.

At the same time that 'A4' is written against item 2 on the script, '2' should be written against item 4 on the preliminary list of scenes for spool A. Then the spool lengths can be cut and the pieces put into the numbered compartments of the editing boxes. If several scenes follow one another satisfactorily, there is no need to separate them for editing, unless, as sometimes happens, the first frame of each shot is noticeably lighter in tone than the other frames. If such is the case, it may be necessary to cut out the light frames.

When all the scenes have been sorted into final order, splicing up is a straightforward job. With the reel on one's right, the length of white waste is first wound on; then the main title, joining the top edge of the first picture frame to the end of the white leader; then the first frame of scene 1, and so on.

When the whole film has been spliced together, with the black trailer at the end, it is rewound on to another reel and is ready to project.

A bit of scraping may be avoided when joining on the leader and trailer, thus: the end of the white waste is spliced to a 4 in. length of black waste, shiny side to shiny side, and the 4 in. black waste to the first picture frame, shiny side to shiny side; and the same kind of thing is done with the trailer.

The film must always be handled only by the edges; finger-marks show up badly on the screen and are not easy to remove from the emulsion side; film cleaner, or carbon tetrachloride will usually get them off the shiny side.

Film cement is very volatile, so the cap should never be left off the bottle for any length of time.

To hold the attention of the audience it will seldom be possible to make use of every foot of film that passes through the camera. Each scene projected must say something, but it must not go on saying it after the audience have absorbed the idea. One hates to throw away good film, perfectly exposed, but if it isn't necessary to the theme it should be cut.

Each scene should bear a clear relationship to the scenes that precede and follow it, unless there is an obvious break in sequence; this may be indicated by a sub-title or by a second or two of black-out.

It is seldom satisfactory to put together a succession of long-shots, or a succession of medium shots; it is better to break them up by interposing a few close-ups, even if they were not made at the same time. But continuity must be preserved: a scene of a boy wearing a cap must not be spliced in between two other shots of him, purporting to be taken at the same time, without a cap. A left-to-right panning shot should not be followed by a right-to-left pan; and a cut in the middle of a panning shot almost always looks wrong.

As far as possible there should be continuity of tone; that is to say, a dark scene should not be put between two light scenes, unless, of course, it is done to achieve some particular effect. This continuity of tone business can be very tricky with colour, for it sometimes happens that of two spools exposed under similar conditions, one will be processed to a normal tone, while the other will be bluish or perhaps weak in contrast.

Good editing is very much a matter of good taste. Straightforward presentation in chronological order will usually be best in a simple film, but if the editor has ideas for dramatizing a sequence or reassembling a few shots to give a humorous twist, there is a lot of fun in doing it, and the family will, as likely as not, appreciate the effort.

Chapter 16

PROJECTING

IN ESSENTIALS a cine projector is very much like a cine camera working in reverse.

When the *camera* is pointed at a brightly lit scene, the lens projects a small image of the scene on the sensitized film; the light coming through the lens is then cut off for a fraction of a second by the shutter while the motor moves the film on and brings the next frame into position in the gate; then the operation is repeated.

In a *projector* the small picture on one frame of the film is very brightly illuminated and the lens projects a magnified image of it on to a screen. The beam of light is then cut off by the shutter while the film is moved on, the next frame is projected, and so forth. But the introduction of a powerful lamp just behind the film brings complications; and the projector uses reels that hold much more film than camera spools or magazines.

Fig. 73 shows the essential parts of a projector, and fig. 74 the inside of one particular type – the Ampro. The motor is driven electrically, and as the light from the lamp B must be concentrated as far as possible on the tiny area of the film in the gate F, it is helped by a reflector A and a condenser C.

Many 8 mm. projectors however use lamps which incorporate a reflector (see fig. 81) and do not require a condenser or separate reflector. These lamps, working on a low voltage, have very compact filaments, are relatively cool running, and give an intense light.

Projector lamps almost always work at a lower voltage than the mains, the current being cut down by means of a transformer or resistance. This may be a separate unit but normally it is built into the projector. If a transformer is used, the projector can be run off A.C. mains only; resistances can be used with either A.C. or D.C., but they waste a certain amount of current and they get hot.

The claw mechanism for moving the film forward frame by frame, G, is similar to that of the camera, but the shutter D

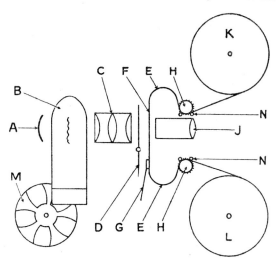

Fig. 73. This diagram shows the working parts of a 16 mm. silent projector. Key to the lettering: A—Reflector; B—Lamp; C—Condenser; D—Shutter; E—Film; F—Gate; G—Claw; H—Sprocket wheels; J—Lens; K—Supply reel; L—Take-up reel; M—Fan; N—Rollers.

cuts the beam of light not only while the film is being moved on from one frame to the next, but also twice during the time each frame is being projected, i.e. forty-eight times per second instead of sixteen times. This is to prevent flicker. The shutter may be a rotating disc with segments cut out, somewhat similar to the camera shutter, or it may be in the form of a barrel with wide slots.

Fig. 74. The working parts of an Ampro 16 mm. projector. The lettering corresponds with that of fig. 73. The shutter on this model is of the barrel type mentioned on page 120.

Fig. 75. The Kodak Brownie 8 mm. projector, inexpensive and efficient, uses an 8 volt, 50 watt lamp, and weighs only 9¼ lb. Here the projector, with 200-ft. reels in position, is ready for action.

Fig. 76. Pathescope Princess, an inexpensive projector of unusual design which provides for projection of 9·5 mm. cine and stills; companion to the Prince camera (fig. 9).

The projector lens J usually has a big aperture and no diaphragm; it is normally of longer focal length, e.g. 2 in. for 16 mm. film instead of the 1 in. used in the camera. But just as the modern tendency is towards wider-angle lenses in cine cameras, so many projectors are fitted with lenses of shorter focal length than formerly; e.g., $1\frac{1}{2}$ in. for 16 mm. and $\frac{3}{4}$ in. or 20 mm. for 8 mm. projectors. This results in a bigger picture for the same projector-to-screen distance (see table on page 143). Some projection lenses have variable focus, so that the size of the projected picture can be made bigger or smaller without moving the projector. This can be very convenient where rooms are small and the distance from projector to screen is limited.

The projector may be designed to take only the smaller reels of film (400 ft. for 16 mm., lasting sixteen minutes; 300 ft. for 9·5 mm., lasting twelve minutes; or 200 ft. for 8 mm., lasting sixteen minutes) or it may take larger reels, such as 800 ft., 1,600 ft., or even 2,000 ft. for 16 mm. The most popular reel for 8 mm. is that which holds 400 ft., lasting just over half an hour; smaller reels involve the bother of stopping the projector more frequently to change reels and re-thread the film.

The reels may be linked with the motor by belts or they may be gear driven. There will be a switch, or preferably two, for the motor should be switched on before the lamp, and the lamp switched off before the motor. This is to make sure the fan is working at full speed for a short time before and after the lamp is burning. The lamp gets intensely hot and its life will be prolonged if this precaution is taken. The average life of a projection lamp is only about 25 hours, and replacement is expensive – round about £2 in many cases. As a further precaution, it should be a firm rule never to move the projector while the lamp is switched on. And always have a spare lamp available.

The projector may have some or all of the following features:

Integral Case: If the projector is built into the case, it is only necessary to fasten on a lid in order to transport it – a convenience, and an economy, for a separate case might add to the cost of the projector.

Fig. 77. The Eumig P8M projector uses a 12 volt, 100 watt lamp and has an f/1·4 lens. There is provision for reverse projection, stills and power rewind.

Variable speeds: Important if you wish to show profession-ally-made films which run at 24 f.p.s. as well as films made at 16 f.p.s.; useful too when using a tape recorder with the projector.

Framing and tilting: The framing knob or lever enables the precise area of each frame to be projected, and the tilting device avoids packing books under the front of the projector to raise the picture to a screen at a higher level.

Inching knob: This permits the film to be advanced by hand one frame at a time as a check that it has been threaded correctly.

Rewind: This enables the film to be rewound on the projec-tor; it may be operated manually or more rapidly by the motor.

Single frames: Some projectors provide for showing single frames as 'stills', a heat filter being interposed in front of the lamp to prevent damage to the film.

Reverse projection: this permits the film to be shown back-wards and makes it possible to repeat a sequence on the screen without re-threading.

Fig. 78. G.B. Bell & Howell Movie-master 8 mm. pro-jector, with lamp-house cover re-moved to show the Tru-flector lamp (see fig. 81). As with the Brownie and some other projec-tors, the carrying case is an integral part.

Fig. 79. The lens of the Moviemaster is here swung to one side to facilitate threading the film. 400 ft. reel in position. It is essential that the loops are properly formed and maintained during projection. Note the white film leader.

Pilot lamp: This assists threading without switching on the room lights.

Re-forming of loop: Some projectors have a device which re-forms the lower loop if this should fail during projection.

Cleaning of gate: It is important to be able to get at the gate in order to clean it – preferably after each film; dirt lodged in the film track may cause scratches. Some projectors permit cleaning of the gate even while a film is being projected.

Sound coupling: The projector may provide for sound coupling with a tape recorder, either directly or by means of a separate coupler.

Anything that is quite flat and opaque and matt white will do for a screen; the projected picture will be satisfactory, for example, on a white or off-white distempered wall. But there is a lot to be said for a properly constructed screen that frames the picture precisely with a black border; and if the projector is not very powerful, a silver or beaded screen will give added brilliance for a small and compact audience. The screen must be taut and must be constructed so that it will stand or hang quite flat.

Prices of projectors vary enormously, and it is wise to look at the window displays of dealers and to study the advertisements in *Amateur Cine World* in the light of the details just given before deciding which model to choose. There is no reason why a second-hand projector should not be satisfactory if bought from a reputable dealer who will give some sort of guarantee with it. If possible it should be obtained on trial, and the appropriate instruction book should accompany it. The lens J and condenser C and reflector A should be perfectly clean, the pressure plate in the gate F unscratched, and there should be no accumulation of dirt on the claw G or sprocket wheels H or the rollers that hold the film on the sprockets N. The machine should run reasonably quietly and there should be a good draught from the fan.

It is important that the loops on the film are maintained during projection, that the film winds itself smoothly on to the take-up spool L, and that the catches on the spool arms hold the reels securely. And, of course, the projector should throw a clear, steady picture, without any wavering, on a screen of adequate size at the screen distance that will normally be used. It is wise too to get a model for which spare parts are readily available.

The threading of the projector should present no difficulty; the method varies with different machines, but the instruction book, or one demonstration, will make things clear. Fig. 79 shows the way loops are usually formed. With reversal film and commercially made films, the emulsion side must be towards the lens.

When the film has been threaded, the motor should be run for a second, or the inching knob used, to make sure the

Fig. 80. The inching knob, between finger and thumb, moves the film forward frame by frame to check that loops are correct. The lens in this picture in the Filmovara, with variable focal length between 20 mm. and 15 mm.

claw is engaging and that the film is being wound on to the take-up spool. It is most annoying to find the film lying in a heap on the floor at the end of a reel, and it can cause considerable damage to the film.

When everything is ready the projector should be run without switching on the lamp until the end of the leader is in the gate (the white leader makes this easy). The lamp is then switched on just as the title is about to appear. At the end, the lamp should be switched off before the black trailer runs out; the sudden glare of the white screen at the end of a film can be very trying.

Before films are shown to an audience, the screen should be erected at a comfortable height, the chairs arranged in suitable positions, and lengths of flex disposed so that people will not trip over them. This sounds elementary, but it is important to avoid fuss or commotion. In a small room it may be best to project from corner to corner. The projector must, of course, be on a really firm support or the picture will wobble on the screen.

With a beaded or silver screen, anyone sitting very much to the side of the line of throw will see a poor picture; but if seats are placed in front of the projector they must be arranged so that heads do not get in the way.

The lens should be examined to see that it is clean and not misted over, and the motor run for a minute or two to get precise framing on the screen and to warm it up. It is a good idea, in order to get the focus right and avoid frantic adjustments as the first title appears, to run a short length of film before the show begins. And there should always be near at hand a spare reel (in case the film should break), a spare lamp and a spare belt.

The instruction book will give directions about care of the

Fig. 81. The Atlas Tru-flector lamp, 22½ volt, 150 watt. Lamps of this type have a very compact filament and built-in pre-focused reflector. They are cool-running and give a brilliant performance in 8 mm. projectors without condenser or separate reflector. The valve-type base ensures accurate positioning.

projector. If the projector requires to be oiled (and some of the modern types do not) it is best to use the oil recommended by the manufacturer and to apply it a drop or two at a time as directed; too much oil may get on the film or splash on to the lens. The gate must be kept scrupulously clean and any tiny scraps of emulsion adhering to the pressure plate removed with a wooden scraper; metal must never be used. The sprocket wheels and rollers should be cleaned occasionally.

The lamp should be examined now and again. If it has blackened, or if the filament has lost its original shape, it is probably nearing its end.

It is well worth while taking pains over projection. A couple of reels may represent a year's output, with hours of filming and editing. It is truly a pity to spoil the effect for want of a few minutes' attention to the projector and careful arrangement of the room where the pictures are to be shown.

Chapter 17

SOUND

FROM THE earliest days of moving pictures it has been a convention to accompany the showing of a film with sound. At first there was a tinkling piano strumming mood music to match the scene on the screen. Gradually, as the cinema became more popular, the piano was replaced by an orchestra. Then came the cinema organ and almost simultaneously, at the end of the 1920's, talking pictures. So it is understandable that if a film is shown cold—without music or commentary—to an audience of more than three or four, something seems to be lacking.

With a family film in the home, the family themselves will probably supply sufficient commentary. Even a musical background may be a nuisance unless it is very subdued. But with a less intimate audience a prepared commentary or musical accompaniment will give the entertainment a more finished air. There is the advantage too that sub-titles will not be needed.

However while the spoken word should give information necessary to appreciate the film, it should never tell the audience things that are obvious. For example, if the scene is the approach to a country town, it is reasonable to say, 'Now we are coming to Evesham', but that comment would be unnecessary and irritating if immediately after it we saw a prominent road sign with the name, 'Evesham'. Similarly the comment would seem out of place if, before we saw Evesham or the approach to that town, there were non-significant scenes such as a picnic party or a couple of close-ups of people.

There are four ways in which a film may be accompanied

by sound: (1) A commentary may be spoken by the projectionist or a friend as the film goes through; (2) Music may be supplied by gramophone records; (3) Commentary and/or music may be supplied from a tape recording; or (4) Sound may be recorded on the film itself, either optically, as in professional films, or by means of 'stripe', which means that the film is given a magnetic track similar to that used on tape, and the sound is recorded and reproduced simultaneously with the showing of the film by a projector designed to do this.

First, the live commentary. This is not as simple as it may seem, and unless care and thought are given to it, the talk may degenerate into an uneven series of interjections; the story relating to one scene may last longer than the scene itself or, on the other hand, it may come to an abrupt end because the projector demands attention; it isn't easy to fix a lost loop, or even faulty focus, and at the same time keep one's mind on an impromptu explanation of the picture. So it is a good plan to arrange for one person to look after the projector and another to tell the story, and for the commentary to be prepared in advance and rehearsed at a trial run of the film. In fact, except for very informal occasions, the commentary should be written out beforehand, with cues to link it with the picture.

Gramophone music can be a satisfactory accompaniment in the home, but the gramophone should be operated by someone other than the person at the projector. One virtue of a musical background is that it tends to hide the sound of the projector, but the projectionist, with the noise of the machine in his ears, is not in a good position to judge whether the volume is too loud or not loud enough. Twin turntables are an advantage; with them it is possible to match the mood of changing scenes by fading one record out and another in, the appropriate portions of the records being marked with a wax pencil.

The gramophone can be used in conjunction with a spoken commentary, provided the music is faded to a low level when it is desired to say something, and boosted up a bit when it has been said. Music must always be unobtrusive. The criterion

131

is that it should not be noticed by the audience; they will be aware that there is music, but generally speaking they should not be able to say afterwards what the music was. If they can, either the music was too insistent, or the film was uninteresting. Popular records which everyone will recognise should be avoided; they amount to an invitation to the more exuberant of the audience to hum or whistle or even to mark time with the feet.

A tape recording can provide an excellent accompaniment to a film, and is the most popular method of doing this. It isn't difficult to get the picture and the tape commentary to start together; a cross scratched on the film leader just before the picture begins will serve as a signal to switch on the recorder, which will have been run to a point where the commentary starts. But the projector and the recorder are unlikely to keep exactly in step unless they are linked.

Almost all tape recorders maintain a constant speed while being played, but a projector is liable to increase its speed as it warms up; so unless the projector runs at precisely the same speed when the recording is made and when it is played back with the film, the commentary may lag behind the picture or run in advance of it. However, sound and vision can be kept reasonably level if the speed of the projector is reduced or increased for a second or two when this happens. And it is wise to word the commentary in such a way that timing need not be precise; instead of saying, 'Here we see some of the little pigs', say, 'There are lots of little pigs,' and it won't matter if the words come a second or two earlier or later than the picture.

Some projectors, such as the Eumig Imperial (fig. 82), have provision for mechanical linking with a tape recorder. A loop of the tape from the recorder is extended to pass over a lever which governs the speed of the projector, so that if the projector goes faster or slower than it should, the governor is operated to control its speed to that of the tape machine. For other projectors which do not include a built-in control of this kind, there are linking units which serve the same purpose.

Fig. 82. The Eumig P8M Imperial projector has a built-in sound coupler. When the tape from a tape recorder is linked with the projector, as here shown, sound can be recorded and later played back in exact synchronisation with the film.

Although the degree of synchronism obtained by this loop method is quite satisfactory for commentary or music, it is not easy to make it precise enough to match spoken words with a picture showing the lips of the person speaking, i.e. 'lip-sync.'; but there are ways of getting round this difficulty. The first-person commentary in a documentary or story film is one method: the person shown on the screen tells what is happening as though he is soliloquising, or recounting the incident in retrospect; now and again he, or another character, speaks a sentence, but with his face averted so that the lips are not seen, and then the narrative continues.

An advantage of the linked tape recording is that it may include both spoken commentary and music and also effects

133

noises, such as the sound of the sea, thunder, a passing train, footsteps, a door shutting, a car hooter, or even a crash. (A collision between two cars, for example, might be portrayed by pictures of two cars approaching each other followed by a few seconds of black-out with suitable noises.) Sounds of this kind would have to be added to the tape from recordings previously made, usually by mixing commentary, music and effects noises provided by a tape on a second recorder. This is because with most machines when a sound track is made on the tape any previous recording is wiped out. But some recorders have provision for superimposing sounds on top of a recording already made; and there are in fact dodges for doing this even with recorders not designed for it.

The next stage beyond sound on tape (s.o.t.) is 'stripe', which is the recording of sound on a magnetic track on the edge of the film itself. This is most commonly done on 16 mm. film, but there are 8 mm. projectors, such as the Circesound, which provide for it. After the picture on the film has been processed, the film is sent away to have the magnetic track added, and the commentary is recorded by the projector in the same way that it would be with a tape recorder.

The obvious advantage is that if the recording is made with perfect synchronism, it will be reproduced that way. The disadvantages are that stripe projectors are expensive, and there is not at present uniformity in their design. The sound head (which records and reproduces the sound) on one projector may be in advance of the gate, so that the sound for any given frame is recorded some inches before the frame is projected, or the sound head may be placed some inches after the gate. This doesn't matter if the film is always to be shown on the same machine, but it means that a film striped in one projector may not reproduce satisfactorily on a projector of a different make.

The optical recording of sound on film (s.o.f.), which is the method used on professional films, is a matter beyond the scope of the amateur. When amateur s.o.f. films are made the sound is almost always added professionally, often from preliminary tape or disc recordings. But many amateurs like to have a sound projector in order to show sound films borrowed from libraries. There are plenty of these on 16 mm. and 9·5 mm., but not on 8 mm. Sound projectors are fairly expensive.

A word of warning about gramophone records. They are copyright, and while they may be played as much as you like to accompany film showings in the home, royalties become due if they are copied or used for public showings. That is why amateur cine societies who want a musical background to a film often obtain the services of a young composer to create suitable music and a local music society to record it, or to record music the copyright of which has expired.

Chapter 18

SOME PRACTICAL HINTS

IF YOU CAN'T afford to buy both a good camera and a good projector to begin with, get a good projector and a cheap camera. The cheap camera may have faults – you can exchange it if it has – but a poor projector may ruin every film you put through it.

* * *

The camera should never be taken on the beach when sand is blowing. A little grit in the motor may put it out of action or cause erratic running, and an overhaul may be expensive. The camera should not be left exposed to strong sunshine for any length of time. If on a tripod, during a pause in filming, a handkerchief may protect it. Apart from the risk of fogging, the heat might affect the film, and the camera too.

* * *

If the camera is not being used for several months, it is a good plan to wind the motor occasionally and let it run down.

* * *

If there is spray in the air when filming by the sea, the lens should be protected by a filter. A ×2 green or yellow filter would be suitable with black-and-white stock, and a 'haze' filter for colour film. The filter should be examined frequently and cleaned if necessary.

* * *

Rain does not photograph well, but a wet day may be indicated by cutting in shots of raindrops splashing in a puddle, drops falling from a wet umbrella, dripping macintoshes, a rain-splashed face, water surging along a gutter, reflections in a wet roadway. The lens must be kept dry, and if the camera gets wet it should be dried before it is put back in its case.

* * *

When the atmosphere is hazy or misty, the scene should include some person or object of interest within a few feet of the camera, and quite sharp, to create contrast. Long shots without foreground interest will be merely ghostly. A meter reading should be taken on the nearby object, and the background left to take care of itself. A 'haze' filter will help matters, or a pale yellow with black-and-white stock.

* * *

Distracting detail in the background may spoil a picture: a strange child gaping at the camera; a tree apparently growing out of somebody's head; an undertaker's sign in a street scene; patches of light showing through dark trees. Because movement always attracts the eye, attention may be diverted by a small figure running in the distance, a flapping curtain, someone on a cliff a quarter of a mile away waving a towel, or a branch swaying at the top of the frame, when the real interest of the scene is in the foreground.

* * *

The direction of movement of a figure may appear false on the screen if the camera position is changed in relation to the figure. If, for example, a shot of someone walking from right to left and out of the frame is followed by a shot of him *taken from the opposite angle* as he continues in the same direction, the second shot when projected will seem to show him returning from left to right. The golden rule is: 'Exit left of frame – enter right of frame.'

* * *

Part of a scene will often say more than the whole. A close-up with out-of-focus background may have more atmosphere than a medium shot that includes a lot of things that have nothing to do with the subject. And a two-second shot of an onlooker will be just as interesting and more effective than a shot lasting six or eight seconds.

* * *

'*Post hoc, ergo propter hoc*' ('After this, therefore because of this') ceases to be a fallacy in cine. If one shot shows A throwing a stone, and the next shot shows B with his hand to his head, the audience will assume that the stone hit B.

* * *

Shots taken through the windscreen of a car add variety to a film, but the windscreen must be clean and the camera close to it. The camera should be rested on something firm, if possible, but 'freehand' shooting will often be satisfactory.

* * *

When shooting from a moving train, preferably through an open window, the camera should be held in the hand, the swaying of the train being counteracted as much as possible.

* * *

A scene containing a number of people, such as a crowd or even a group of three or four, will be more effective if filmed from a height, e.g., from a first- or second-floor window. Cut in a few close shots if possible.

* * *

When something has to be filmed at really close quarters, a positive spectacle lens in front of the ordinary camera lens will serve as a supplementary. It may be held in position with bits of adhesive tape. With the camera lens set for infinity (or with a fixed-focus lens), focus will be sharp when the distance from the object to the supplementary lens is the same as the focal length of that lens.

* * *

If a camera or projector is taken into a warm room from the cold, the lens is liable to become misted over. This would give an unpleasant fuzzy picture. So the lens, or the camera, should be kept warm by carrying it in a pocket or under the coat. The projector should be run for a minute or two, some time before it is to be used, to dispel any moisture on the condenser lens.

*   *   *

When a film suffers from edge-fogging – a creeping in of light at the edges of the picture, particularly near the end of a spool – the fault is not necessarily that of the processing station. It may have been caused by allowing the film to loosen on the spool when loading or unloading the camera, or during transit. The camera should always be loaded and unloaded in dim light, and the end of the exposed film should be stuck down with a bit of adhesive tape or otherwise secured before it is posted off for processing.

*   *   *

If you wish to pan with a telephoto lens, pan very slowly indeed, or use 32 or 48 f.p.s. instead of the usual 16 f.p.s. And whenever you pan, work from left to right if possible rather than from right to left.

*   *   *

Finally – it is worth repeating – when you get any new apparatus or try out a new type of film, always read the instructions – every blessed word of them.

APPENDIX

Film Speed Ratings

ASA and Weston Master III	..	100	80	64	50	40	32	25	20	16	12	10
Weston Master II and earlier models	..	80	64	50	40	32	25	20	16	12	10	8
B.S. log ..	..	31	30	29	28	27	26	25	24	23	22	21
DIN	..	21	20	19	18	17	16	15	14	13	12	11
Scheiner ..	..	32	31	30	29	28	27	26	25	24	23	22

F Numbers & Relative Exposures

If the value of the light passed by the lens at f/16 is 1, then the approximate value at other apertures is as shown below:

F number			Relative value of light passed
2			64
	2·2		50
		2·5	40
2·8			32
	3·2		25
		3·5	20
4			16
	4·5		12
		5	10
5·6			8
	6·3		6
		7	5
8			4
	9		3
		10	2½
11			2
	12·5		1½
		14	1¼
16			1

Effect of Filters
on Various Colours,
Using Black-and-White Film

Colour of object	Colour of filter to render lighter in tone	Colour of filter to render darker in tone
Yellow	Yellow, green, orange	Blue
Green	Green, yellow	Red
Orange	Orange, yellow	Blue
Red	Red, orange	Green, blue
Blue	Blue	Orange, yellow, red, green

Depth of Field

Gauge of film and aperture with normal lens	Everything will be reasonably sharp within the limits shown below when the lens is focused upon:			
	4 ft.	6 ft.	10 ft.	20 ft.
8 mm. at f/1·4 9·5 mm. at f/2 16 mm. at f/2·8	$3\frac{1}{2} - 4\frac{3}{4}$	$5 - 7\frac{1}{2}$	$7\frac{1}{2} - 15$	$12 - 70$
8 mm. at f/2 9·5 mm. at f/2·8 16 mm. at f/4	$3\frac{1}{4} - 5$	$4\frac{1}{2} - 8\frac{1}{2}$	$6\frac{3}{4} - 20$	$10 - \text{inf.}$
8 mm. at f/2·8 9·5 mm. at f/4 16 mm. at f/5·6	$3 - 5\frac{1}{2}$	$4 - 10$	$6 - 30$	$8 - \text{inf.}$

At smaller apertures (e.g. f/8 or f/11) the depth of field will be greater.

Series-Parallel Switching

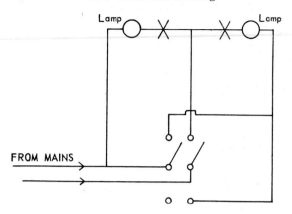

Wiring diagram for series-parallel arrangement of two lamps, using one double-pole double-throw switch. Switches may also be inserted at the points marked × to allow one lamp to be used without the other for preliminary examination of the subject.

Title Card Distances

Approximate area covered by 8 mm., 9·5 mm., or 16 mm. camera with normal lens.

Distance from camera to title card	Area covered
15 in.	$5\frac{1}{2} \times 4$ in.
18 in.	$7 \times 5\frac{1}{4}$ in.
21 in.	8×6 in.
24 in.	$9\frac{1}{2} \times 7$ in.
27 in.	$10\frac{1}{2} \times 8$ in.

Projection Distances

Distance from projector to screen	Approx. width of picture with 16 mm. film				
	20 mm. lens	1 in. lens	1¼ in. lens	2 in. lens	3 in. lens
10 ft.	4 ft. 8 in.	3 ft. 9 in.	2 ft. 9 in.	1 ft. 10 in.	1 ft. 3 in.
12 ft.	5 ft. 6 in.	4 ft. 6 in.	3 ft. 0 in.	2 ft. 3 in.	1 ft. 6 in.
15 ft.	7 ft. 0 in.	5 ft. 8 in.	3 ft. 9 in.	2 ft. 10 in.	1 ft. 10 in.
20 ft.	—	7 ft. 6 in.	5 ft. 0 in.	3 ft. 9 in.	2 ft. 6 in.
25 ft.	—	—	6 ft. 3 in.	4 ft. 8 in.	3 ft. 1 in.
30 ft.	—	—	7 ft. 6 in.	5 ft. 8 in.	3 ft. 9 in.

With 8 mm. film the picture will be half the width given above; with 9·5 mm. film the picture will be four-fifths the width given.

Choice of Lighting

Position of main source of light in relation to the subject	*Sunlight*
Frontal (i.e. main light behind the camera)	Result in black and white rather lacking in contrast; all shadows will be vertical. Satisfactory for colour if glare does not cause screwing up of eyes. Beware of overexposure.
Half-way between frontal and side	Simplest for black and white, and satisfactory for colour if the sun is not intense.
From the side	With hazy sun, quite pleasant; with a low sun the effect can be dramatic. Reflector desirable for close-ups if light is strong. Will need a bigger stop than frontal lighting.
From the rear	Tends to glamorize; figures will be outlined in light but rather lacking in detail. Avoid sky background. Lenshood essential and additional shielding of lens desirable. Open up two stops more than for frontal light.

Dull day	*Artificial light* *
Best if light is very poor	Satisfactory if lamp is definitely higher than subject. Very low lamp will give fireside effect. Level lighting would give flat result, like flashlight stills.
Generally best	Generally best; lamp should be two or three feet higher than subject.
Satisfactory if light is fairly good, but beware of underexposure on a really dull day.	Tends to be dramatic.
Success depends on value of stray light or reflected light reaching faces	For special effects only. Rear lamp, high, is more useful as subsidiary lamp to put gleam in hair. Lenshood essential.

* A fill-in lamp at camera level is assumed. This should be farther away from the subject than the main lamp, e.g. $1\frac{1}{2}$ times as far.

INDEX

146

For every amateur cinematographer

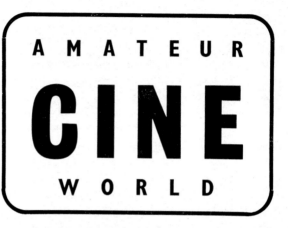

2/- monthly. Annual subscription 30/-

One hundred packed pages of advice, news, hints and views by experienced movie-makers, a guide for amateur producers to current releases at the local cinema, a "how I did it" article by the maker of a prize-winning film, pages of readers' opinions, gadgets, problems, detailed impartial tests on latest apparatus. Cameras and camera-work, ideas for film themes, projection and projectors, silent and sound, tape, film, disc and magnetic stripe . . . all aspects of home movies are covered in *Amateur Cine World* No wonder it is known throughout the world as "the amateur's bible".

Amateur Cine World, 46-47 Chancery Lane, London, WC2

Amateur

MOVIE-MAKER

FOR EVERYONE WITH A MOVIE-CAMERA

AMATEUR MOVIE-MAKER is a monthly magazine with a whole new slant on how to think up, photograph and edit your own movie productions. It is crammed with bright, practical information for every home-movie fan and semi-professional film maker.

Includes detailed do-it-yourself construction projects for professional-type equipment you can assemble and use at home. For instance: You can learn how to build an animation stand to film your own animated cartoons, or how to make a simple "effects box" to fit right over your camera lens and add effects that will give your films a true professional touch. It tells you how to add musical sound background to your films with the construction of a twin turntable unit, or you can learn the advantages of recording your music and sound on tape. AMATEUR MOVIE-MAKER will constantly bring you the newest techniques and the easiest ways to master them.

In addition, AMATEUR MOVIE-MAKER will keep you supplied with a constant stream of ideas on what to film and how to film it.

2/- monthly. Annual subscription 30/-

Fountain Press, 46-47 Chancery Lane, London, W.C.2